Reg Smythe:
Creator of Andy Capp
"My Dancing Bear"

Reg Smythe:
Creator of Andy Capp
"My Dancing Bear"

Hélène de Klerk

Creators Publishing
Hermosa Beach, CA

Table of Contents

Prologue

"He was my dancing bear," Reg said, "because of him I was wanted everywhere."

Reg could never believe how he, in his own words "a short-arsed little bloke with a stammer," could be attractive to people. And yet he was handsome, funny and vulnerable in turn. Early on he handed over his dance card to Andy and became the willing wallflower.

Reg loved words and like most creative people, when he found a phrase which worked he used it over and over. The Dancing Bear analogy was one. But it had echoes of both Andy and himself; a bit of a novelty who could also make an audience slightly uncomfortable while it laughed. Reg, too, was a bit of a novelty. A largely self-taught man, he became one of the world's best known cartoonists through the creation of a work-shy, amoral little character who evoked equal amounts of love and hate.

At the height of the cartoon's popularity Andy equalled Schulz's "Peanuts" fame; the cartoon was syndicated to over 1400 newspapers worldwide, with fans from Adelaide to Yokahama. Reg won the prestigious Cartoonist of the Year Award five years running; the Andy Capp image endorsed everything from Kit Kat to Post Office Savings Bonds and it inspired a TV series and musical in the '80s. He died in 1998 but today Andy is as popular as ever, the cartoon produced by a team of three, all of whom readily acknowledge Reg's genius.

As his niece it is difficult for me to be objective; like most women who knew him I adored him and, if you wanted to keep him happy, which we all did, you accepted that you would always take second place to that stroppy little sidekick of his, Andy Capp.

— Hélène de Klerk

Chapter 1

THE BRUSH dipped into the china pot by his side as the figure slowly came to life on the board. First the black, jutting bottom, then the legs, short, with turned out, dancing feet; last of all, the hatching strokes on the all consuming cap. Reg only glanced up when the mug of tea appeared, the short, sweeping movements continued, swiftly inking in previously pencilled outlines. Like Andy, he had given up the cigarettes years before, but it was hard not to imagine the cigarette smoke wreathing upwards from the ashtray.

There was little change in his working routine during the months before he died, nothing to suggest that his life was coming to an end, other than the conspiracy of silence he imposed, and the total lack of interest in anything other than Andy.

Reg drew in what was called the den, a small dark room on the side of the bungalow, which, despite its many chairs, did not invite company. It had the closed look of a gentleman's club, with its hard leather sofas and its artexed walls covered with awards and honours. It was a gentleman's club with only two members, Reg and Andy. And yet, when you were invited to join him, there was a feeling of intimacy impossible to recreate anywhere else in the house.

From this seclusion he created Andy's world, with its daily run ins with bartenders, rent men, policemen, referees and the never ending sparring with Florrie. His creative output went on day in, day out, with little distractions; contact with the outside world was through fan letters and requests for original cartoons, which he replied to immediately with a personally written note, rewritten several times before sending.

The den had solid black beams; the story was it was timber retrieved from an old Far East sea vessel. Reg sat near the fireplace, flanked by two small windows with blinds, which he increasingly preferred half drawn as his eyesight deteriorated.

He sat in what was a left over chair from a much earlier suite, a chair that never looked as though it belonged in the room. Reg refused to have anything different and its status as a magical seat grew with the years. Yet when I sat on it, awkwardly, shortly after Reg died, I found it surprisingly hard and unyielding. I can hear him telling me ...

... *I don't like to be too comfortable, makes me uneasy. Doesn't quite sit, if you'll excuse the pun, with the Independent Chapel work ethic which was drummed relentlessly into me ...*

There was a little pouf at his feet, equally worn, where he placed his prepared drawing boards and other papers while working. The table by his side was packed with pens, inkpots and bits of stationery stuck in metal cans. Some of them he no longer used, such as the mapping pens, but they remained stuck in painters' pots, echoes of his earlier studio life in London.

The larger table on his other side had an overfringed lamp, which served to deter visitors from full view, together with a pile of fan letters and the ubiquitous mug of tea. This tea was only ever in two states, either steaming hot or with a faint skin of tannin as it cooled; the required drinking condition, just half a degree below scalding, was only rarely achieved because of Reg's total absorption in his drawing.

He would have teased me about using "ubiquitous"; he had a self-educated man's suspicion about any word he was unsure of. Such absorption was remarkable as the television was always switched on. Sometimes it was daytime TV, but mostly it would be one of the two or three films that he had selected that morning from his huge selection of both recorded and pre recorded videos. This collection, numbering well over a thousand, was housed in a little bunkroom. They were nearly always old favourites, ones that would not tax his concentration and would play quietly, like an old friend, while he drew.

All time favourites included "All the King's Men," "Teacher's Pet," and "Gentlemen's Agreement," "Pat and Mike," "Citizen Kane," "Seven Brides for Seven Brothers" and, among his top five, "Love Me or Leave Me."

... I like the relationship between James Cagney and Doris Day in the film — captures perfectly the way a man can act so stupid because of a woman ... her singing is wonderful, too ...

Reg drew on his lap, left-handed. I was always fascinated by his hands, although large, the solid, square tipped fingers had a powerful symmetry, while the thumb joint on his left hand had become a hard, bulbous mound of muscle. He worked on a 12 x 10 hardwood board every day, adjusting an angle poise lamp as he needed. Early in the mornings he cut his required number of white Daler drawing boards to size on a guillotine, exactly five. This was his personal commitment, never less than three, and rarely more than five boards, to be worked on during the day. He had already written down his ideas on bits of paper.

The ritual acted as a kind of limbering up exercise, much like a dancer or boxer. Mornings were for ideas, reading papers, old joke books and sifting through the hundreds of odd cartoons and clippings, which were kept in makeshift boxes in the cellar. He used these to help kick start his own imagination, looking for what he wanted to say through the humour.

... A good cartoon is more than just telling a gag, it should be a story in picture form, with the telling as important as any punch line. I like to set up the scene in the first two frames, put the gag in the third and let the fourth frame go soft ... having Florrie look at the reader with an I told you so expression, or Andy kicking up his feet on the way to the pub. A favourite would be Andy and Florrie, in silhouette only, walking home together ...

Picking up the lapboard and fixing the white card with two large bulldog clips was his signal for drawing to start; it sometimes began before lunch, which was invariably eaten alone, on his knee, with the TV news to punctuate his eating.

It seemed Reg could have been living in a one-room flat for all the interest he took in the rest of the house. The elegant lounge and dining room were only used during family visits and the large, ornamental garden, with its pond, never. His involvement in the house was to move paintings around; he had collected many paintings over the years and it gave him pleasure, particularly when a new one was bought, to rearrange them all. It was as though he was a museum curator, which was how he described himself in the last months.

The rest of the house hummed around him as he drew: his first wife, Vera, with her regimented programme of cleaning and washing, accompanied by the loyal housekeeper who hoovered and polished about the den. Visitors were discouraged and the telephone always answered by Vera in her Sunday best voice; yes, he's in and thank you so much for calling but he couldn't possibly attend/open/speak at any opening/event/dinner/talk show. The press would telephone, more in the early years of him returning to the North East, and particularly if there was some new statistic on

6

wife battering or drinking. He would sometimes give a comment, or a rare interview, but practically none at all in the last years.

... The stammer always held me back. I remember years ago at a cocktail party given by The Mirror Managing Editor Hugh Cudlipp and I said how difficult I found talking to the press, he told me to tell them no, to be different. And it worked, I was known for saying no, so people bothered me less and less ...

The drawing would continue uninterrupted, with a steady supply of tea, until around 6 p.m. when he would stack the finished cartoons on the leather sofa opposite and go and wash up. He would have a beer, or perhaps a gin and tonic, and then read a paper, or watch TV news, until Vera called him for dinner.

Reg continued to receive plaudits for the standard of the cartoon; the growing number of international awards joining the grinning five "Oscars" in the den. He enjoyed the acclaim from fellow cartoonists but he had long become used to what he called "the knockers," resigning himself to the vagaries of public opinion and political correctness which either praised or damned the cartoon strip.

... They don't get it do they? It's not about now or how I think it should be, but how it was. And the relationship between Andy and Florrie says as much as anything does about what goes on between men and women. I still think Florrie is the nicest, wisest woman there is, I created her as well as Andy remember ...

But plaudits and fan letters could not lure him from his den and any attempt was deflected with a gentle refusal. Even once eagerly anticipated trips to London to deliver his batches of cartoons had been replaced by a private courier service.

... A quiet life I guess, but that's the way I want it now, a steady rhythm with no sudden upsets. You'll know why ...

How will I know, I wondered? The unchanging routine was important to him, a routine which I never felt to be stifling until those last few months, when absorption became obsession and he retreated behind Andy for good.

Chapter 2

WRITING ABOUT Reg once he died had seemed easy but as time has sped by the words and memories grew landlocked. Now the need to write from my own memory has resurfaced, as much for me to understand my creative matrix as his. I began by sifting through an old box of photographs, not sure what I wanted as I went through the images of bleached beaches and smoke filled restaurants. My eye was caught by a group of lean children playing in back streets, alongside a professional portrait of Reg, cigarette smoke curling, after collecting his first award as Cartoonist of the Year.

I scrutinised both, trying to see the link between the laughing, Mediterranean-looking 8 year old and the assured looking man with his brilliantine hair. The boy's laughter was unexpected because of what Reg had always described as a brutalising childhood with his paternal grandparents. He reserved particular venom for Grandmother Smyth who, he announced, made sure they all suffered.

"All" was my mother, Lily, and his younger brother, Jim, immortalised in our family as "Our Poor Jimmy." But the venom he expressed for Grandmother Smyth thickened with fresh intensity each time he spoke of his mother.

I had never heard a woman called a bastard before and I grew hot each time he repeated it, remembering her kindness to me. I wanted to tell him how much he looked like her, how similar in their shared sense of fun and child like vanity. He did not want to hear it, preferring his time warped memory and damning her never forgotten act of abandonment in a tight, bitter voice.

... What sort of woman leaves her husband with three kids? Don't you believe it when she tells you it was an act of impulse, and she just meant to give him a shock. She meant it, already had someone else lined up ...

The Smyth's lived in Hartlepool, a once grand sea port on the North East coast with its own Saxon saint, but eclipsed over time by its flashier, more prosperous Victorian sister, West Hartlepool. Reg said the Smyths clung hard to the fringes of respectability; they were regular churchgoers and, unlike most of their neighbours, owned their own house. His grandfather James had worked in the shipyards and there were four grown up children, all living at home. The fifth was Richard Oliver, Reg's father, and a bit of a waster by all account, with boot black hair and eyes. He had married Florence Pearce because, it was suggested, he had to and Reg, the surviving twin, was born in 1917.

He was born when the Great War had been mutely raging for nearly three years. Reg's father was a boat builder and one of the protected few left behind, while his mother, Florence Pearce, was also from Hartlepool. She was the youngest of 13 and born just as her mother's fondness for naming her daughters after flowers was exhausted. Young Florence spent most of her early years being looked after, grudgingly and with varying ability, by the older flowers.

... Know how I got to be called Reggie? When she went to register me, they asked what he was called and she replied, Reggie of course, not knowing it was a nickname for Richard. She didn't even give me a middle name ...

Reg was followed by Lily, another pair of twins, Harry and Laura, who seemed to make little impact on him or anyone else, dying before the age of 2, and finally, Jimmy. Although born in Hartlepool, the family quickly moved to Sunderland, where Reg's father found work; money was still short and I recall my grandmother's tales of wheeling the children about the neighbourhood, offering to read palms or tea leaves for sixpence.

Reg, however, shared little about that time except for an incident that appeared to be seared onto his retina.

... I must have been about 7 or 8 when she started sending me over to the cobblers. She would give me a message for the bloke on where they were to meet but would add, in dramatic hushed tones that if a woman came in I was to buy some laces ... the poor bastard hung himself not long after and I think it was because she told him she was pregnant ...

He remembered, too, rows about money and of a constant, furious knocking at the front door. It was during one of the bitter silences following a row that Florrie disappeared; a few days later his father returned to Hartlepool, three children in tow. Another retina scarring incident came during a confrontation between his parents.

Reg's father said he would take Lily and she, Florrie, could have the boys. She wanted neither. I often wondered if that painful rejection led to Reg's continuing doubts over his own paternity, fuelled by Jim's white blondness and rapidly growing legs.

... I could never be sure if he was my father – although now, late on, when I look at that rather doughy face with the black hair, and even blacker eyes, it seems to me he was – poor, spineless sap ...

Despite Reg's description of living with the Smyths as being pretty miserable, he came off slightly better that the other two. He learned to keep on Grandmother's right side by accompanying her to Independent Chapel, every day and twice on Sundays. Such diligence was rewarded with indifference; if you weren't noticed you didn't get slapped, and you weren't asked to do much. No such luck for Lily or Jimmy; none at all as it turned out.

... You know, I never remember my father sticking up for us. He was beholden to them, I suppose, for taking us in but once we got there, he just abdicated from any parental responsibility. I seem to remember he spent a lot of time in the pub or playing football, always with his cap on, except for Sundays when he swapped it for a bowler hat and that was it ...

The wage packet was the dominating currency in the household; those that worked got first place at the dinner table and always the best cut of meat; grandparents got the remaining slices, the girls and aspiring workers got the corned beef and the lower rankings got the gravy and bread. The workers, Uncles Percy and Tom, had napkins at the table and were waited on by their sisters. Reg and Lily cleared up after all of them.

Contact with Florrie was sporadic after returning to Hartlepool. She had also returned to the town and was living with a man who had children of Reg's age. Their meetings, always clandestine, were conducted at school gates and around street corners, when she would sometimes give him tuppence and extract cross your heart promises not to tell anyone he had seen her.

... Grandmother always called mother the actress, not because she liked to make a scene, but because she often sang publicly in the local pubs. She had a good voice, strong and melodic. The songs she sang were about birds living in gilded cages or with clipped wings ...

The pecking order among working class children was footwear and, according to Reg there were at least four rankings. Top of the heap were those with shoes, then came boots, followed by plimsolls or canvas and, finally, the barefoot brigade.

... I sort of scraped in with a sixpenny pair of Plimsolls from Woolworths, courtesy of my Uncle Percy ... but even that degree of conformity didn't make me fit in any better. As I remember it, school thought I was a lost cause, I was left handed to boot and so they put me at the back of the class. Actually it was a blessing because that's where the heating was ...

Reg stayed on at school until aged 14, lucky to get jobs as a sign writing apprentice and grocer's assistant before joining the formidable Mrs. "One Spike" Walker as butcher's boy. He told me she got the name because of her ability to fell a beast on slaughtering day with one swing of a spike through its forehead. And he was still going to Independent Chapel, drawn as much now by friends like Pud Jones and a girl called Esther as any need for grandmother's approval. Esther, a slight and wasted looking girl, gave him the best birthday present a 16-year-old boy could ever have. She may, too, have been only the second woman to break his heart.

... I'd been in love 14 or 15 times by the time I was 16. I was in love with the drama of it all, used to go out with a girl just to have the drama of breaking it off. I got that from the pictures, we all did ... that was where you learned about romance ...

Florrie continued to exert an influence; Reg was the first to swap the Smyth's doleful comfort for lodgings, which his mother shared with a one-legged trumpet player. And, although not comfortable, its easy come, easy go philosophy proved a heady brew for the 17 year old.

... I found out it was okay to lie in bed, not to worry about finding the rent money ... but I was still hanging round street corners, and it ended up as much a prison as living at grandmother's ...

It was about this time that Florrie changed her name to Pat, on her sister Daisy's insistence that the name wasn't glamorous enough to fit in with the singing group she was forming. Daisy was one of the oldest Pearce girls, her steely face matching a determination to make a name for herself. Florrie never kept up with Daisy's big time plans for the small time band, but she did keep the name Pat.

Reg spent almost two years on the dole before spotting an army recruitment poster which asked "Why not play tennis around the world?" He had never seen anyone play tennis before. He joined the Royal Northumberland Fusiliers in 1936 when he was 19 and signed up for 12 years. It was to be the last time he saw his father.

... He decided to come and see me just before I left and invited me down one of his favourite snooker halls. He racked up the balls for a game called 'Loser pays' and we started playing, me telling him, in between turns, about going to Egypt and him telling me 'we haven't seen much of each other – pink in the middle pocket – be a good lad.' His last words to me were 'Loser pays.'

Army life was everything Reg hoped for. The mornings were spent training, and the afternoon relaxing or playing games. He learnt to play tennis and enjoyed the camaraderie among blokes who had escaped the same stifling, dead end backgrounds he had. His army nickname was Vic, after a famous horse trainer of the day, Vic Smyth, which Reg reckoned was fair enough given the number his mother had backed over the years.

He spoke warmly of the companionship in his unit, of friends like Knocker Knowles who looked out for him, making sure he got the lion's share of food and the cleanest shirts. The army was full of skinny, motherless boys; what was it about Reg, which made people want to take care of him I wondered? It was a quality he shared with Lily and Jimmy, with their bruised fruit good looks and overwhelming need for approval. For Reg, the Army went a long way to answering that need. He continued to believe it was the best thing that had happened to him.

... The army was everything to me at that time, it gave me food and shelter, friendship, self respect, even a sort of personality ...

Army life in pre-war Egypt was uneventful, the long hot days punctuated by an occasional visit to a Cairo brothel while on leave. Even in those business-like settings Reg noted the drama between the sexes.

... I usually went with the same girl but one visit she was unavailable. She saw me coming out of a room with another girl and slapped me, hard. I was astonished that she'd mind ... but I enjoyed the drama, of course ...

There was no chance of home leave, but most soldiers had no reason to return home, anyway. The only way was on compassionate grounds, a frequent occurrence, which alerted Reg to an opportunity to earn some extra money. His clear, firm handwriting had already gotten him the job of inking in names on grave markers, and now there was a chance to extend that talent. The first thing soldiers bought when they were returning home was a camel-hair suitcase; keen to impress folks back home they took up Reg's offer to initial their luggage. Soon he was initialling briefcases and other insignia, as well as writing letters home for soldiers.

Suddenly he found something he was good at, and his confidence soared. He began drawing caricatures of sergeants and CO's for his friends' amusement, most of them by his own admission pretty awful, but they demonstrated a firm hand and an eye for the comical. He reached new heights when he submitted four cartoons to W, the Cairo-based Forces Magazine, and had every one accepted. Reg began to imagine a different life when he was demobbed, sharing his hopes of becoming a sign writer, even a commercial artist, with army friends. He knew it was a dream impossible to remember, even less to admit, if he had stayed in Hartlepool.

During those quasi-lethargic days, of chasing Italians and being chased up and down the Western Desert, letters took on great significance. Reg received regular mail from Florrie, often sent with a welcome pack of cigarettes, and eventually letters from Lily who had just forgiven him for leaving. But he yearned for something more to fill the hot, idling afternoons, and readily agreed to become pen pals with a girl from Hull, writing:

... I hardly know what to say, my pal was asked to produce a pen pal and I was tickled to death when he picked on me and – well, here I am. Introductions were never one of my strong points, and I don't even save stamps or collect autographs, but nevertheless I really do have a yen for girls called Vera. I draw and play tennis an awful lot but even so I have time to kill so you see I really do need someone to write to. I have lots to write about but somehow I can't get round to it, a letter from you, Vera, would help me ...

This gauche letter was the start of what was to be a seven-year correspondence between Reg and Vera Toyne, who became his wife. Vera was a year older than Reg, office photos showing a small, confident looking woman with a handsome face.

When the War started, it came as a shock for everyone and for Reg in particular, who was suddenly switched to a tank demolition team. Their goal was to try and demobilise any German tank they came across, and pinch parts belonging to the better equipped German tanks. According to Reg he never saw an angry German, just disinterested or tired ones.

... When the Germans headed for Tripoli they left a small squad behind, we captured five and one of them got away. My CO ordered me into the desert to bring him back. I jumped out of the jeep as soon as I spotted him, even though my army boots were too big and my rifle had sanded up. Suddenly, the biggest German I had ever seen loomed in front of me, staring as I struggled to put a shell in my rifle, and then went and sat on the jeep bonnet ... we drove back to camp that way ...

I laughed with Reg over these stories many times, but there were other, darker ones, told late at night after two or three brandies. Memories of how he tried to make a whole corpse from bits of fly-decked bodies found out on patrol, and of nightmares from accidentally knocking down an Egyptian child but being too terrified to stop. Oh, and he made

Sergeant, too, where he claimed the hysterical shrieking he was forced to adopt did wonders for his stammer.

The bundle of letters between Reg and Vera grew, their inner lives becoming as important as what was happening everyday. His letters showed an ease with words, a love of style and language which belied his oft stated lack of self worth. He told her of life back in Hartlepool, not of the respectable Smyths, but stories concerning Florrie and her doings, of Jim "the subdued," and of sister Lily with her movie star face, who had escaped to London.

Photographs, too, displayed an inherent ability to communicate directly with the reader. One photograph, a straightforward one of Jerusalem's wailing wall, was captioned: "You can guess what it is. Right." Another photo, this time of some army buddies but not very clearly developed, stated: "and the light wasn't bad and yes, the camera was a good one." It seemed as though Reg was having a conversation directly with the viewer, a style he later perfected with Andy. His photographs also reveal an initial, unfortunate enthusiasm for army business; a picture taken after a local fracas, was captioned: "Black eyes were dished out freely. It was a glorious five minutes."

But letters, written later on in the War, display his growing disillusionment with army life, as he began to fight a bigger battle with his own ennui and sense of hopelessness. He began to use cartooning as a way of fighting back against what he called an air of "God forsook," of miserable surroundings, indifferent days and selfish evenings. Reg quickly realised what made the other soldiers laugh, telling Vera of his attempts to kill time in the evenings.

... I have decorated the Mess with lewd sketches – not by choice – but by request. How stupid. Raphael, da Vinci, Whistler – all these leave our fellows cold. But a drawing of a half-naked, tattered and torn ATS girl, with a medal pinned on her chest, with the caption, 'and then he says accept this, you put up a bloody good fight anyhow' slays them ...

The correspondence between Reg and Vera grew steadily more meaningful and took their relationship far beyond simple pen pals. In these letters they spoke of their hopes for the future and of a commitment to be together once he was demobbed. He reveals his elation at her caring for him, and his fears of when they would eventually meet.

... We have no more decisions to make, we have already made the one. If you can take me as I am, marriage and less glorious, whether I draw or work in a shipyard – all these are incidental. Things will work out. This may sound sweet in theory, but I believe it. The only worry I have is the idea of my disappointing you ...

The last years of the war were hard for Reg, troubled not only by what he saw as an unfair army but by a niggling stomach complaint, later diagnosed as an ulcer. In a letter written in 1942 to Vera he spoke disparagingly about her friend who had stood to attention at the National Anthem, eyes filled with tears:

... You tell me how they all stood to attention with tears in their eyes whilst singing the National Anthem, "all those poor boys who gave their lives" ... the verb is out of place, they didn't give anything, on the contrary they were stuck in and they fought like the devil to keep their lives ...

He began to take pride in being thought of as rebellious, recounting in a long letter how he was demoted back to corporal for some undisclosed misdemeanour, recounting how he felt he was freewheeling into peacetime.

His growing disquiet troubled him; he questioned his own sanity several times, asking why first he loved the army, then loathed it, in another letter.

... And the inconsistency of thought covers more ground than soldiering. Deep down I am religious but I don't like going to church, but I do like coming away from it. I often think that if going to church and wailing makes people good and straight – even though praying is futile, the deception is worthwhile. Sort this out Vera, whilst fire watching some evening ...

What was left of Reg's unit was shipped back to England in 1944, and this quietened his questions, but not his bolshiness. Reg was regularly disciplined for having a dirty rifle or refusing to attend church parade, tension, which aggravated his ulcer and led to him being transferred to a hospital in Edinburgh, before being medically discharged in 1945. His 'finishing school' days, as he called them, were over.

Upon receiving his discharge papers, he headed straight for Hartlepool and a reunion with Florrie, and arranged his first meeting with Vera Toyne.

Reg's mother, Florrie, during her singing days with sister Daisy.

Grandmother Smyth with two of her daughters.

Reg's father, Richard Oliver Smyth, known as "Reggie."

Reg (far left), aged 15, working as a butcher's errand boy.

Vera Toyne at the start of their seven-year wartime romance.

Reg, Royal Northumberland Fusiliers, circa 1937 in Cairo.

Photo from Jerusalem, with a caption that hinted at Reg's future style.

Reg (right) just after enlisting in 1936.

Cartoons drawn by Reg while serving in the Army.
They often appeared in the Forces magazine, W.

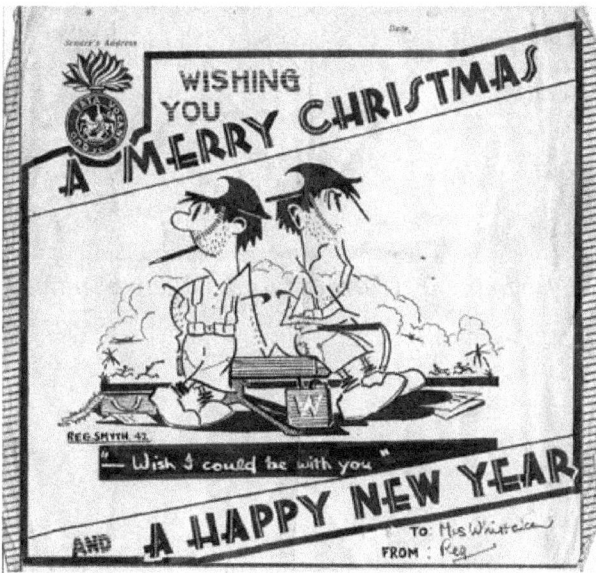

More cartoons from Reg's army days.

His army cartoons were drawn under the pen name "Vic."

Chapter 3

THE ENGLAND Reg returned to was not that different to the one he left in 1936. There were still men hanging round corners, hanging round bus terminals and hanging round stations. This time they wore large, army overcoats, just like Reg. The feeling of sameness was reinforced when he went home. Florrie was now living with Charlie Low, a good-looking foreman from the shipyards whose lackadaisical approach to life suited her perfectly. He was ready to spend his last penny, and anyone else's, on having a good time. For Reg it was like stepping back 11 years.

... You know mother thought I'd gone mad. I was sitting at the kitchen table, musing out the window and I murmured chimney pots a few times. She stared, broke out sobbing and ran up the road to her older sister, crying 'our Reggie's gone funny.' It would never occur to her that being stationed in the desert could change you in any way ...

His morale was lifted when he met Vera; their first date as awkward as any meeting between two people who knew each other inside out but had never met. The time together confirmed their desire to marry, and Vera promised to join him in London once he had found a job and somewhere to live. But first she had to meet Florrie.

Florrie's melodramatic sense of romance was perfectly in tune with Reg's wartime love; for her it was a case of star-crossed lovers, not a man and woman turned 30. She set the scene for their rendezvous, turning her front room in Arch Street into something akin a Turkish boudoir, with scarves draped over the light and perfume sprayed onto the pillows.

They sensed it was the end of the relationship as they had known it; letter writing played such an important part in their relationship, it was difficult to imagine it ending. He wrote:

... This is probably my last letter to you. It is the end of something what started almost eight years ago. A happy ending – and a lovely beginning. Now we have next year, and the next year, and more years after that. And all of them together ...

Vera, too, knew the significance of what was ending, replying:

... I have spent the last hour burning all my letters from you, except a few which marked milestones in our relationship, and I find I have been transported back into the latter part of 1943 when I was looking forward, so much, to your homecoming. Every thought and action was wrapped up in this thought. I was going to say that I wonder, now, how I could ever have felt that way. By 'that way' I mean I wonder how I ever felt that you were, in spite of your letters, someone I didn't know. Now, I feel that there has never been a moment in my life that I have never known you as I now know you ...

Reg was pinning all his hopes on London, his expectations raised with the example of Aunt Daisy, now a successful bandleader and sister Lily, living in splendour in a house called Malmain's Way with a Belgian who had a way with charm and other people's money. But his hopes were dashed in the first few weeks, his acute sense of dignity repeatedly affronted by disinterested would-be employers.

... *Who could blame them? I was one of thousands looking for work and I didn't even have a trade. After a few weeks it was hard to remember how hopeful I had been when I left the army, buoyed up with friends' praise and a sense of what I might achieve. I'd even added an ' e ' to Smyth because I thought it was more classy for an artist ...*

He worked for a while with his new brother in law, Eddy, who ran an import-export agency in central London. It was there he met Mort Bignell, who took an interest in the rather lost young man, insisting on him continuing to draw in his spare time and encouraging his hopes of becoming a commercial artist. As yet Reg didn't think you could make a living out of cartooning. It was Mort who arranged an interview for Reg with the Samuel Cooper Advertising Agency in Central London. I found that letter after he died in an old wallet.

... *This impeccably dressed bloke leafed through my small case of sketches. I remember the deafening silence before he asked me if I drew for pleasure. When I said I did, he told me I should continue doing just that. It was a crushing let down – convincing me I had absolutely no talent and should forget all about drawing once and for all ...*

While he set out with new fervour to find 'proper' work he lived with Eddy and Lily, who helped him enjoy London. They took in shows and films, and through Eddy he learnt to feel comfortable in restaurants. He discovered that eating was something you did for pleasure, for a whole evening, and not as a prelude or an afterthought. Eddy's easy confidence was a revelation to Reg; his refusal to queue, wait or take second best was an attitude rooted in a secure, well to do family upbringing, everything, which had been missing with the Smyths.

... *I was fascinated by his ability to brazen situations out through a concoction of charm and absolute confidence. Once, he'd invited next-door neighbours in for drinks, and, as an inveterate practical joker, had decided to dress up as Lily's 'sister.' He made an incongruous woman in a floral frock, with muscular legs and a vague blue shadow dashed over with talc, but when I said it would never work, he said that even if the neighbours had doubts, they would never be voiced in case they were mistaken ... and he was right. The only other man I ever met like that was Robert Maxwell ...*

Despite the housing shortage in post-war London, Reg found a small flat in Victoria, South London, and telegraphed Vera to join him. She did two weeks later, and found an office job the next day. He, too, found a job with the General Post Office as a temporary clerk, Grade 3. His job was to match the hundreds of telephone tickets to the right subscriber before authorising billing. The mind-numbing work prompted his volunteering for a course in typing, and he was promoted to temporary clerk and roving typist, Grade 2.

They settled into their life together, although Reg's ulcer continued to play up, resulting in a dangerous loss of weight. Photographs show a good-looking, deceptively confident man with a liking for soft, corduroy jackets and a moustache, which more or less stayed with him for the rest of his life. The addition of a beard was, for him, the ultimate two fingers. He still considered himself a rebel.

Every so often they would head back to Florrie's for a weekend, doing the eight or nine hour journey in the first of his prized cars, an Austin 7. During these stopovers the routine seldom varied; he would scour the racing pages with Florrie and put a bet on before popping down for a pint before lunch. Later Reg and Florrie would go off, arm in arm, to the dogs or a favourite pub, like lovers, while Vera stayed home to play cards with Lily or read by the fire.

What he saw on the frequent trips back to Hartlepool fuelled Reg's imagination. Here, life went on as it had between working class men and women for generations. There were the frequent eruptions between Florrie and Charlie, punctuated by dramatic departures and grim silences, usually fuelled by too much brown ale or Guinness. Life revolved, as in a fairground, around a very small circle of pub, bookies, pawn shop and snooker hall.

Florrie gave as good as she got, and very often it was her who dished it out in the first place, marching down to the pub with Charlie's dinner if he was late or pawning his fob watch to settle a racing bill without telling him. She herself told the story of how, irritated by the sight of Charlie's recumbent back on the sofa while she was clearing out the fire, tossed a can full of ashes all over him.

Visitors to the terrace house in Union Road were required to stake allegiance to one side or the other, taking sides, literally, as they sat on one or other side of the kitchen range fender, while Florrie or Charlie took it in turn to pour out their frustrations. All the visitor could do was fix his or her eye on the tin bath hanging from the back door and nod at an appropriate gap.

It was the same tin bath which has been immortalised in the Andy cartoons; like a downmarket Cleopatra, I would take turns to bathe in front of the fire, with Florrie acting as handmaiden bringing in steaming kettles.

Despite these regular set-tos, Florrie claimed Charlie was the love of her life, he was certainly the most like her. I remember an unsmiling man in a black suit, cigarette glued to his lip, who wore a large flat cap and let me dress up in his white silk muffler. This was the raw clay for the characters of Andy and Florrie, although the genders were not so clearly defined. Florrie had much of Andy's bloody mindedness while Charlie had elements, and particular expressions, of the long-suffering Flo.

Their physical appearance, too, like their namesakes, changed over time. Florrie shortened as she filled out, while Charlie became smaller and slightly bowed under the weight of his checked tweed cap, which steadily grew larger as he shrunk in size. But he still had Andy's turned out feet.

Reg knew this world only too well and, while dipping into it, remained as much an observer as always. He renewed his acquaintance with Florrie's family; there was Uncle Harry with his rag and bone cart, "in textiles," said Florrie; a cousin Jackie who liked to collect back doors, and a mysterious "aunt" who apparently had frozen to death in the outside lavatory, and was found to be a man while being laid out. Florrie's friends, too, were like-minded women, lives unfolding on front door steps, unlike their hair, which remained tightly curled and hidden by pudding basin cloths until they went out in the evening.

In his own way, Reg was proud of Florrie's spirit, he had referred to her ability to "marmalise" in one of his letters to Vera, and actively encouraged her liking for drama during his visits. It became his own entertainment, something he could switch off when he wanted by returning to the safety of his life in London.

Reg and Vera were married in 1949, witnesses were Aunt Daisy, who now had her own all-women jazz band, and her husband, Norman Burrows. They moved to North London shortly afterwards, buying a small house in Haringey with a little help from Daisy, who recognised that Reg shared the same drive as herself. Meanwhile, Lily had gone back to Hartlepool to have her baby when Eddy had disappeared and 'Our Poor Jim' had joined the merchant navy.

... At this stage, I had put all thoughts of drawing out of my head; until in 1952 I decided to join one of the many little drama groups ran by the GPO for its staff. I didn't fancy acting, so that just left designing the poster for the staff notice boards. I can still remember the title, 'Flowers for the Living'; I drew the biggest bunch of blooms imaginable to hide the fact that I couldn't draw people ...

But the compliments he received from the drama troupe revived his hopes, and, once again, Mort Bignell drew on his address book to arrange for Reg to see an agent called Charles Gilbert. The agency handled both commercial and cartooning; what Reg saw in the busy studio confirmed his belief that he would never be an artist. He watched as a young boy drew a mouse with such precision and artistry that the mouse came to life, so much so Reg put out a hand to stroke it. He knew he could never match that boy's talent, and told Mr Gilbert he wanted to concentrate on cartooning. Gilbert acknowledged Reg had a talent for comic drawing and responded by throwing down a challenge. If Reg could draw 30 cartoons within the next week then he, Charles Gilbert, would sell them. Reg had earlier embarked on a self-improvement correspondence course called Pelmanism, which instructed students how to "master concentration," and he clearly made good use of it.

... I don't think he thought he would see me again, but for me it was as though a green light had been switched on. I rushed back home and started drawing round the clock, and seven days later delivered my batch of 30 to Gilbert. Exactly a week later, he rang to say he had sold three for three pounds each to a magazine called Living — it was more than my GPO salary for the whole week ...

For Reg the biggest thrill was having someone buy something he had created; he bought a tin alarm clock, one with the loudest bell he could find, and set about devising a system for drawing, which set the pattern for his later disciplined and exacting regime. He regarded this period as one of the happiest of his life, he relished the security from his Civil Service job; he and Vera were enjoying the social life of the capital as it slowly revved back to life after the war. And now he had his dream back.

Letter writing between them was a hard habit to break; during a trip back to see her family in Hull, Reg wrote, and posted, one which acknowledged both his romanticism, and his fear of showing it:

... What a day! Empty, the room is empty, like the day, like me. The kettle is also empty. I had hearts for lunch. I thought of the poor cow. Then I thought of your mother — I mean I thought of you at your mother's place. I think how heartless of you to leave me to

myself, knowing that I am not my own type. I tried to draw, and could not.

How awful, I thought, to be without the woman permanently, I may as well be dead, or in the army – which is the state of being dead. And with these wonderings come the embarrassingly corny clichés. 'I am dead without you' and 'do love you more than myself' All this is old stuff, all this was said, repeated and written many times, from many places – but now with a difference. Once I thought I meant it, but now, I know. And when I meet her at the station, will I tell her thus? Will I hell! This is to let her know there is everything in my 'did you have a seat all the way, darling?'

There was an unquenchable thirst for cartoons after the war; magazines were bright and plentiful, with titles like Reveille, Post, Titbits and Weekend. Editors were almost indifferent to standards in their hunger for a new supply. The few who were genuinely talented could almost name their own price, and depended upon their agents to get the best deal. Reg decided to bombard Charles Gilbert with drawings, this time upping the weekly quota to an incredible 60. His routine was precisely worked out, almost military style. He would return home from the GPO around 5:30 p.m., have tea and almost immediately start drawing, with the alarm clock set to ring every half hour. If he finished one cartoon in 15 minutes that allowed him 45 on the next, and so on, until he had stacked up 60 boards.

... It was amazing, but we still managed to enjoy life; somehow that pressure gave it piquancy, a sort of forbidden fruit, because every minute away was time spent not drawing. Our biggest enjoyment was going to the cinema, and then onto a cafe; but this had to be timed to perfection, because there was an awful lot of wasted time before the feature began, with news, national anthem and adverts. Vera would check with the cinema the actual time the film would start, and we would dash in exactly four minutes beforehand, watch the film and dash back to resume drawing. It was a fun time ...

Pressure of time made it impossible to visit Hartlepool so often; Florrie came and stayed occasionally, always on her own and frequently with more bags than for a weekend stay, but she always went home. From her Reg heard tales of Charlie's latest misdemeanour, or incidents in her neighbours' lives; someone like Annie, who shared her home with both husband and lover, either one regularly seen washing the front door step with Annie pointing out the smudges with her slipper; or of Billy Mac, who had been a school friend of Reg, who took his best mate on honeymoon for "when things got boring."

Florrie's tales provided him with insight into the enduring relationships between men and women, which had no resemblance to the films he enjoyed so much and yet were more fascinating.

Reg kept up his prodigious output of cartooning for an astonishing five or six years, while still working full time at the Post Office. He was now achieving a moderate success, as editors became familiar with his work; Reg put his growing success down to perseverance and sheer volume—he was also very funny. His output was extremely varied; anything would spark off an idea, a rare night out at Haringey Stadium watching speedway racing led to the creation of an accident-prone speedway star Skid Sprocket, a regular cartoon by Reg which appeared in Speedway World and which spawned a series of cartoon books starring Skid.

He had even come up with his first regular strip, The Sparks, a cartoon strip about a young, middle-class couple, which appeared in Midweek Reveille. The Capp hallmarks were already there; the Sparks fought, they fell out, they humoured one another. They were just better dressed.

Reg was one of many freelance cartoonists at that time, artists who earned a good living without being tied to any one paper or magazine. One of the top earners was a cartoonist called Lesley Harding, who drew under the name Styx. He was also handled by the Charles Gilbert Agency, and he and

Reg became friends, his guidance helping Reg to develop his inimitable style.

... Styx could really make his cartoons move; he was known for his ability to create action within static, two-dimensional drawings through concentrating on his characters' fancy footwork. He had them shaking, fidgeting, tapping or kicking, which all helped to enliven the drawings. I started to look at my cartoons that way, asking myself how I could bring in more movement ...

Styx liked Reg's style and regularly passed on work when he had more than he could handle; there were commissions from major trade magazines like Farmer & Stockbreeder, Fish Trader's Gazette and Draper's Record. For Reg it was a tremendous challenge thinking up cartoons, which had some relevance to these mysterious worlds — and very good training once he had to produce daily storylines for Andy.

Styx encouraged Reg to concentrate on movement, but other freelance work for local newspapers also contributed to the development of his style. For the first time readers saw prominent back views in the cartoon frame, instead of figures retreating into the background.

... My lack of confidence over drawing still held me back, I felt I had to compensate all the time. I was working as a freelance illustrator for one or two local newspapers, covering council meetings, and I knew I wouldn't be able to do proper likenesses. I started to draw back views of the councillors; I got to like it, and some people actually thought I was making a political point!

When Reg thought of an idea or a gag that amused him, he often practised drawing actions or objects necessary to the cartoon, like a crane or bike, with tracing paper first. The figures were quite simple; a fan later described these early efforts as deliberately simple so as not to detract from his punch line, Reg replied by saying it was because he could not draw any better.

... I find it so hard to advise budding cartoonists. My own work wasn't all that good when I first started drawing panel cartoons. So when someone sends me his examples and asks me if he should carry

on or pack it in, all I can say is that their drawings generally look better than my own first attempts ...

His collaboration with Charles Gilbert was when the popularity of cartoons were at their height; the cartoon page was often the most popular part of tabloid newspapers, and each strip had a devoted following. Reg's work started to appear regularly in the Mirror's Laughter at Work Column, a selection of cartoons by freelancers, which sat alongside the Mirror regulars such as Garth, Buck Ryan, Belinda, The Perishers and the war-time favourite, Jane.

Not only were Reg's cartoons funny, there appeared an inexhaustible supply. He and another freelancers often vied for the lead spot at the top of the cartoon page until one day the Mirror's cartoon editor called them both in. Fed up with sifting through the thousands of submissions each month, he announced that the one who won the most commissions over the next month would get the job of supplying Laughter at Work permanently. Reg won the contest, but not before increasing his output of 60 cartoons to 80 for the month. He now decided it was time to pack in the day job.

... I was now driving a car twice the size of my boss at the Post Office, and had begun parking a few blocks away from work in case anyone noticed what I was driving. It was madness ... but the security was very hard to let go. I suppose a psychiatrist would say it was because of the insecure childhood, but part of me actually enjoyed working at the Post Office — the drawing was the jam on the bread and butter. I wasn't sure what I would replace the jam with ...

Life was becoming very sweet; he and Vera bought a larger house in Enfield called Tudor Cottage and he was able to fulfil one of his army ambitions — he had a full size billiards table installed in the hall. Trips back home to Hartlepool continued; Florrie was enormously proud of Reg, regularly cutting out his daily Laughter at Work cartoon, now simply called Smythe, and pasting it in scrapbooks until the pile grew too high.

I remember the air of expectancy when Reg and Vera came to visit, starting with the parking space Florrie earmarked in front of the house with empty milk crates, to the shiny, unopened bottle of brown sauce on the new tablecloth. Florrie enjoyed lengthening the distance between the crates as the expected arrival drew nearer, putting on a show for the street.

When a neighbour complained of the empty space during a heated exchange, she thought she would gain the upper hand by threatening to bring out her husband. Florrie squared up to this threat in the back lane, white sheets flapping, and told her to bring him out too. She would flatten them both.

But the best part was always the anticipation; the good humour generated by Reg's expected visit evaporated like air from a tightly held paper bag once they arrived. Florrie would drink too much and the air would crackle with unacknowledged friction until Reg would cut his weekend visit short.

... The idea was so much more attractive than the reality. I loved the going much more than the arrival; just like during the War when I spoke of only being happy coming away from something ... mother could be tremendous company, and that was great for the first few hours and then it all went wrong ... she couldn't keep it up ...

Andy Capp was conceived in a lay-by during one of these unsatisfactory trips back from Hartlepool.

Florrie, on her wedding day to Tony Ritson –
immortalised as the rent man.

Reg with Florrie on one of his frequent trips back home.

*Reg gaining inspiration from an evening in the pub
with Florrie and friend.*

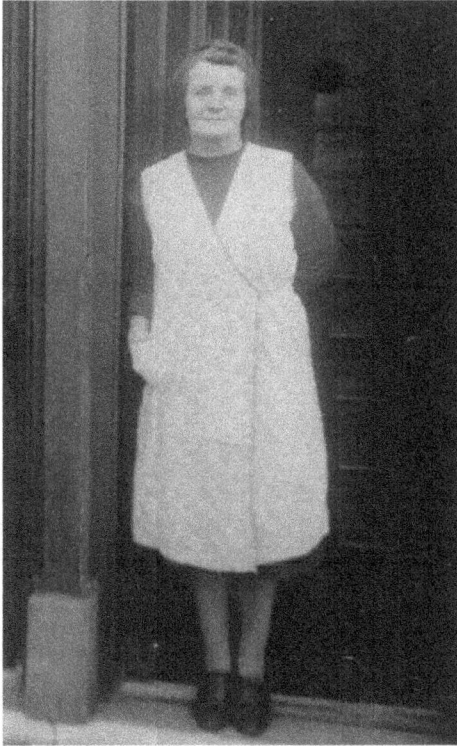

Florrie, hair in curlers, prior to an evening out.

Florrie with me and Charlie Low –
and his distinctive turned out feet!

Vera and Reg, playing with me, in their North London home, in the early '50s.

Reg and Vera starting to enjoy his growing success.

Reg at work in one of his many home "studios."

"The Sparks," a cartoon Reg drew for the Reveille in the mid '50s.

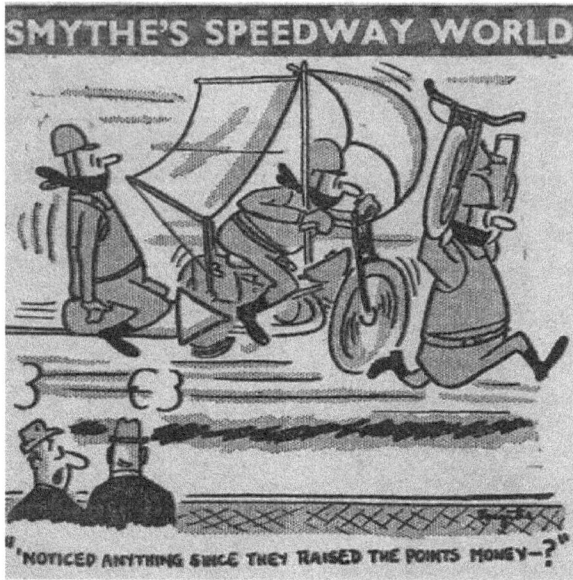

Reg's creation, "Skid Sprocket," was a regular in The Speedway World.

*Series of cartoons created by Reg for agent
Charles Gilbert from the late '40s onwards —
and which established Reg as a good jobbing cartoonist.*

" YOU'RE SOFTENING HIM UP — HE'S
BEGINNING TO FEEL SORRY FOR YOU "

*Now a freelance for The Daily Mirror, Reg's
work regularly appeared on Laughter at Work page.*

"I CAN'T REMEMBER THE NAME BUT THE FOOTPRINT IS FAMILIAR"

"I CAN'T REMEMBER THE NAME BUT THE PACE IS FAMILIAR"

*Same gag, different settings — something
Reg was never ashamed of using.*

Chapter 4

WHEN REG JOINED the Daily Mirror in 1955, it had a circulation of 2,500,000 and its funny page was the most widely read in the UK. Their cartoons were heavily influenced by the hugely popular American heavyweight supplements, and at the start the Mirror featured cartoons that shamelessly imitated the leading American strips. Such was their success that The Daily Mirror set up its own commercial studio with a full time team of cartoonists.

To begin with, Reg felt overawed by the other cartoonists' success, he never thought his contract would last more than six months. In fact his collaboration with the Daily Mirror lasted 42 years. From the start of his cartoon career, Reg did his own writing, drawing and lettering. This was unusual, most cartoons were a collaboration between a writer and an artist; some strips had as many as five or six different collaborators, and most cartoonists certainly farmed out the laborious job of lettering.

... None of it was hard work to me, so I never thought of having anyone else involved, I supposed I liked to be in control. But I didn't think anyone else could possibly know Andy's world, and how I wanted it to look, so I did it all myself. In the end, I was more familiar with his world than my own, and how could I explain that to anyone?

Although Reg had given up his Post Office job to concentrate full-time on cartooning, his routine was relatively unchanged; he still spent time in the evenings thinking up ideas and making notes, so when he arrived at the Mirror's studio he could get straight on with drawing. The pattern of Reg and Vera's married life was now fixed, he drew while she took care of business.

Despite growing demands at work, Reg continued with his visits back to Hartlepool, finding inspiration from the seemingly unchanging world of Florrie and Charlie. He gradually noticed they were slowing down, even their sporadic outbursts of violence towards each other lacked a convincing edge. Only in their outings to the pub afterwards, arm-in-arm, seemed comfortingly familiar. A favourite venue was The Seaton Hotel in Seaton Carew, a seaside holiday town always on the brink of a boom. This was the sanctuary to which Florrie always fled when the rent man knocked.

I remember playing a bit part in her drama, her admonishing me not to cry, dabbing my dry eyes as we legged it down the back lane while the rent man banged on the front door.

But gradually Charlie became greyer and Florrie wrote to let Reg know that he had been diagnosed with cancer. He died in 1957, and Florrie was suddenly adrift and frightened. When Florrie was unhappy, she inevitably turned to one of her sisters. This time she went to stay with Rose in Blyth, a busy shipping port further up the North East coast.

The stay in Blyth turned into one of Florrie's indeterminate visits. The reason may have been more to do with a lonely widower called Tony Ritson than any change of sea air. Florrie was now in her late fifties and, after 20 turbulent years with Charlie Low, was now homeless. Encouraged by her more practical sister, Florrie and Tony married two months after meeting. Their wedding photo shows up the incongruity of the pairing, the diminutive Tony Ritson staring anxiously at the photographer, with a stage-managed Florrie dwarfing them both with her brand new hat and smile.

Tony could not have been less like Charlie Low; where Charlie was happy-go-lucky, Tony was measured and considered. Charlie liked nothing better than being in a pub; Tony's spare time was spent creating a 6ft replica of a cruise ship from matchsticks. Florrie hated that boat, which she prophetically nicknamed Titanic.

Her marriage to Tony foundered after barely a month, as much by Florrie's appetite for battle as his unsuspected stinginess. Lacking a worthy adversary, she returned to Hartlepool alone, save for her wedding ring and the name of Ritson. The surname sounded posh, she thought, and so did Reg. Tony was to be immortalised in the Andy Capp strip as Percy Ritson, the rent collector who has a soft spot for Florrie.

Soon after her return, Florrie met one of Charlie's former workmates in the local pub, and quickly formed a bond with someone who she thought had some of Charlie's sparkle. Percy Gibson was to prove neither as sparkling or so accommodating as Charlie, but he did have the advantage of having a club foot, a handicap which provided Florrie with an immediate advantage in their confrontations. Their attraction was cemented by shared interests in betting and going to the pub. She moved into his terraced house, and wrote Reg to inform him of the new arrangements, uncannily like the old.

Morning began with the fire being lit, summer or winter, and Florrie would first paste Reg's cartoon into her scrap book, before spending a few rapt hours studying the day's races, hair tightly curled in metal rollers. Percy would run messages to the local shops if she hadn't baked, and morning break was signalled by the first of several Newcastle Brown

Ales being opened. Florrie would gauge the day's luck by playing cards, always a game of patience, which she would continue playing until she was reassured she had given her horse the best possible omen.

The hair would stay covered until it was time to go to the pub and Florrie began to get ready, always with full makeup, applied with all the precision of a Maori rugby player. She would spit into her mascara box to work up a thick cream and then paint a livid cupid bow on her thin lips, smacking them hard together with a popping sound before dusting them lavishly with powder and reapplying the bright red colour.

There was always an air of dread when the evening paper arrived, had her horses won? If not, she would accuse anyone who was at hand of putting the mockers, or evil eye, on her. If she'd won she always shared her winnings; money was never that important to her, winning was.

Satisfied that life seemed to have resumed its usual pattern in Hartlepool, Reg began to enjoy his life at The Mirror, and the friendship of the Studio team, men like Jack Dunkley, Ian Gammidge, Fred Parker, Ken White and Len Gamlin. Gammidge, a cartoonist with a loyal following, remembers a forgotten age of drawing boards, where artists would arrive in suits and ties and swap their jacket for a white coat before drawing. The banter was fast and furious, he recalled, based on a mutual sense of regard for each other's talents. Reg was always the quiet one in the group, but if he was uncertain about his ability, it never showed.

The studio was eager to meet this Smythe bloke, someone who had single-handedly made the Laughter at Work column all his own while still a freelance contributor. This was confirmed when the Mirror stopped calling it Laughter at Work, and published Reg's cartoons under his own name—with the extra "e" of course. At last he could draw anything he thought funny, no longer tied to thinking up ideas solely around work.

Reg found it fascinating to be part of a daily newspaper's incestuous world, soaking up the atmosphere in the White Hart pub, a famous haunt for newspaper people known affectionately as the Stab in the Back or as Reg later penned it during Maxwell's era, the hand round the throat.

... In some ways it was like the early days of the army, there was the camaraderie between the men, all of us against the studio head or director ... we all respected each other, but never allowed anyone to get too big headed. I was interviewed once, and the journalist described me as looking like a dashing Spanish count – god, I loved that – the boys in the studio asked me how she had spelt count. That sort of joshing was better than any compliment ...

Settled into Studio life, and now accepted as part of the team, Reg and Vera headed back to Hartlepool for what was to be the usual few days stay with Florrie and Percy.

They had barely recovered from the seven-hour journey, when Reg received an urgent telegram from The Daily Mirror Cartoon Editor, Bill Herbert. Reg remembered it was a long telegram.

"Sorry to interrupt your holiday, but Mr. Cudlipp needs a cartoon to appeal to Northern readers. You are wanted straight away. Come back quick. That's the newspaper business!" The rest as far as cartoons go, is history.

Hugh Cudlipp was the then legendary Managing Editor of the Mirror Group, and, as a former journalist, he had a shrewd sense of what Mirror readers wanted. He believed a regional cartoon for the Northern editions was his answer to falling sales following the Suez Crisis of 1956, and the paper's support of Labour leader Hugh Gaitskell. He summoned Bill Herbert and asked about the background of their in-house cartoonists. Being the only Northerner, Reg got the job.

... I found my head frighteningly empty on the way home ... all I could think about was Mother and Percy, and our trip to the dog track that last night in Hartlepool. The idea began to form of a man and woman and their daily life ... no more than that. I thought that

would do for starters, a rough draft to hand in while I could come up with the 'real thing' ...

Reg pulled into quite few cafes on the journey back to London, jotting down any ideas he could think of on one of his Piccadilly cigarette packets. As soon as he reached home he started sketching, the images of women and men he had just left earlier that day, women with pinnies and men with caps and thick belts holding up trousers. But the name eluded him. Over breakfast the next morning, he played around with the name cap, cape, Capp. That seemed okay, he liked the names Bill and Fred, wanting something short and snappy to go with Capp.

He eventually decided on Fred Capp, but as Reg tinkered with the sketches, pulling the cap further and further down over his character's eyes, he thought of what sort of man he might be. He'd be a right pain and a definite handicap to anyone, that's for sure. The pun was hard to resist, Reg inked in the name "Andy Capp," put the drawings in his case and set off for the Mirror offices.

... Even now I almost blush when I think of such a corny name ... I certainly thought Bill would groan and hand it back. I couldn't see him in his office so, relieved, I left the drawings on his desk and went back to my room. I was amazed, he liked it, and felt confident enough to show it to Cudlipp. He decided to run it the following week in the Manchester edition of The Mirror, it was considered a short term thing. I went back to thinking up ideas for my Laughter column slot ... a proper cartoon, I thought ...

Andy began life as a single frame cartoon, created to replace Reg's usual slot at the top of the regular Laughter page in Northern editions of The Mirror. Despite being an immediate success with Northern readers, its humour was still regarded as too regional for the South, so Reg still had to come up with the Laughter panel for the Southern editions.

Andy Capp made his first appearance in the Manchester edition of The Daily Mirror on 5th August, 1957, but it was to be another eight months before he was unleashed on the rest of the country.

Reg struggled to keep up his standards on two very different cartoons until it was agreed, with some trepidation, to let him concentrate on Andy for all editions of The Mirror. It was printed in London on 14th April, 1958, and, like a slow burning Catherine Wheel, began as a talking point with newspaper staff, before catching fire with the Mirror readers.

Suddenly the editor noticed circulation was rising in all editions of The Mirror, and within five months the readers' postbags were bursting. Mirror readers' letters during that first year record the fizz of approval from readers who had never encountered anything like Andy before.

What most of them asked was how did Reg know their "uncle, dad, brother, husband" so well? A Mirror report on viewers' letters dated June 16, 1958, summarised the readers' comments:

"Readers feel they know Andy Capp (often husbands), and what they think of Smythe's creation is very flattering—with one or two exceptions—they say in unison Andy is terrific, he's tops, he's a real tonic, he sends me, this from a 20 year old." (This was the start of the Teddy and the bebop phase). "Keep up the good work" was the general consensus from readers.

A few extracts selected at random: "Andy is typical of the Northern countrymen who sees himself as the boss, the clever one who is never wrong ... I'm a lonely widow and don't get many laughs but how I enjoy Andy ... "

"Our neighbour is a right Andy Capp; talking to my husband while his wife was painting the outside of the house he said 'of course I don't like to see the missus up a ladder'" ... "Andy is a complete replica of the fathers of the children I teach" ... "My 'Andy' advises me when I am cutting or carrying in bags of shopping" ... One critic asked if couldn't Smythe create a funnier character, "someone with a basis in reality?"

Part of Andy's success was that it was based on reality, everyday life for huge chunks of the population who found the Capps' daily concerns amazingly like their own. Someone had found what they did important enough to put it on record, and, in laughing with it, made their lives seem more important, too.

What people had been used to laughing at were cartoons about middle- or upper-class people, the odd labourer or working class were generally portrayed as cockney spivs or eccentric "characters." Men were nearly always hen-pecked.

The concerns of the working class or, in Andy's case, a class all its own with absolutely no desire to change status, had never been so realistically portrayed. Worries over finding the rent, dodging the mother-in-law, enjoying a drink, going to the club and getting the better of your missus was Andy's everyday diet—and also of a whole section of the population who either lived like Andy, or dreamt of doing so.

... I couldn't believe the response at the beginning ... the praise was overwhelming, can you believe someone actually comparing Andy to Homer, another epic hero I think Malcolm Muggeridge called him. I was tickled pink, yet I felt a bit of a fraud. They were praising someone I knew all about, people I could smell, they were that real. All I had to do was come up with the punch line every day – and to begin with that was what it was, a vehicle for telling a gag ... the Andy and Florrie figures were very similar to others I had been drawing ... Andy was taller and thinner then, and I put in lots more detail of his clothing, the belt round the trousers, for instance, the war overcoat. Florrie, too, had a variety of patterned frocks and hats, they were both younger, see ... Andy was often drawn just in trousers and shirt, with a thick belt round his middle, while I had Florrie wearing a variety of dresses. She was seen quite often without a hat or curlers, just as I depicted the 'lasses' in later cartoons ...

Florrie was very proud of her son's growing popularity; she revelled in the fame by association, saying yes, of course she was the Florrie in the cartoon but in truth finding little to identify with in Florrie Capp's blind subservience. She continued to cut out the cartoon and let the pile of newspaper clippings grow on the sideboard, welcoming the interest from the local newspaper, Hartlepool Mail, and allowing them to take photographs of her in her metal curlers and headscarf, much to Reg's annoyance.

... It was the reference to my father that sickened me ... I'm sure it was based on my husband she was quoted as saying. "Oh yes, he liked his drink and a bet, too". How the hell would she know? Of course there were elements in there, he was like a hundred other blokes I knew from Hartlepool, but he lacked the edge and the bite which I gave Andy. Mother had enough for both of them ...

As Andy bawled into life, Florrie took her first and only foreign trip during 1958. She went to stay with Lily, now reunited with husband Eddy, at their holiday home on the Belgian coast. Percy came too.

She loved to tell the story of her first boat trip, her loud shout of 'Land' while standing on the prow of the deck, and I loved to hear them, particularly with all her exaggerated gestures and facial expressions, asking her to repeat favourite ones over and over again. Always the actress, Reg commented bitterly.

Reg's growing success was a major topic during the holiday, but nothing compared with the publicity the little horror was beginning to generate in newspapers and magazines. It is probably hard now to imagine the public reaction to the cartoon strip; anarchic characters like Johnny Speight's Alf Garnett, Ian Pattison's Rab C. Nesbitt and Bart and Homer Simpson have dulled Andy's impact, but in the late '50s, the cartoon was revolutionary.

The success was to give Reg a life he had never imagined, and with growing international recognition, a way of life which threw an intensely private man into a very uncomfortable spotlight. He had now also met Jean during one of his outings, introduced by a mutual friend at one of the popular drinking clubs in London's West End. She was a beautiful 32 year old, a Londoner with a passion for the cartoon who did not know who Reg was, but thought him the most handsome man she had ever seen. Jean was to spend the next 40 years or so as part of his life.

Jean gave Reg the total devotion that Vera had supplemented with other things as she realised that drawing would always come first. Jean knew that, too, but she chose to become as obsessed as Reg; she looked out for ideas in newspapers and magazines, typed up rough outlines of his gags, and was always ready to fuel his store of stories on long evenings spent together.

Rough sketches for "Andy Capp."

Daily Mirror

Dear Mother,

Just a line to tell you
that we will be coming up
on Friday. Leaving here
early, and hope to arrive
for lunch - around 1.pm to
to half past.
I'm looking forward to it.
There was a call from
Tyne Tees Television while
I was out yesterday - must
be about another proposed
show at Newcastle, so I'll
probably be up there again
before I know it.
See you
Love

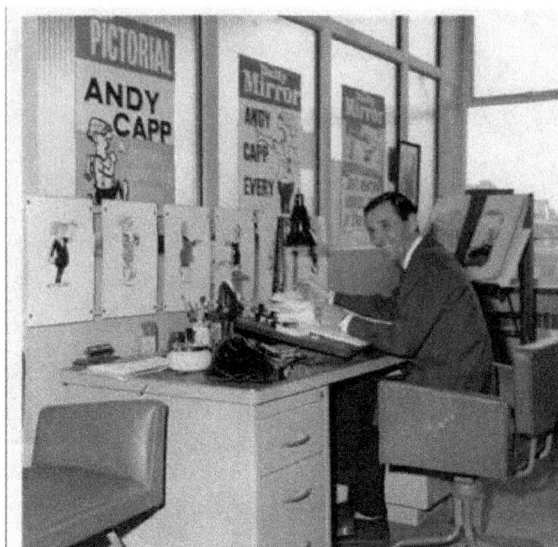

Reg in The Mirror Fleet Street Studio.

Travelling to South of France in his beloved MG.

First "Andy Capp" cartoons from 1957 – then single frames.

Another early "Andy" – with longer, leaner figure.

Andy Capp, early '60s, and using a broad Northern vernacular, which Reg later softened.

Reg and Jean, who met in 1960 and formed a relationship that was to last nearly 40 years.

" Yer new dress came in fifth "

"LOOK, LAD, IF YER DON'T GO TO SCHOOL, YER WON'T LEARN TO WRITE — THEN 'OW ARE YER GOIN' TO FILL IN YER POOLS ? "

Single format cartoons from 1960s — still using broad Northern slang, and later dropped

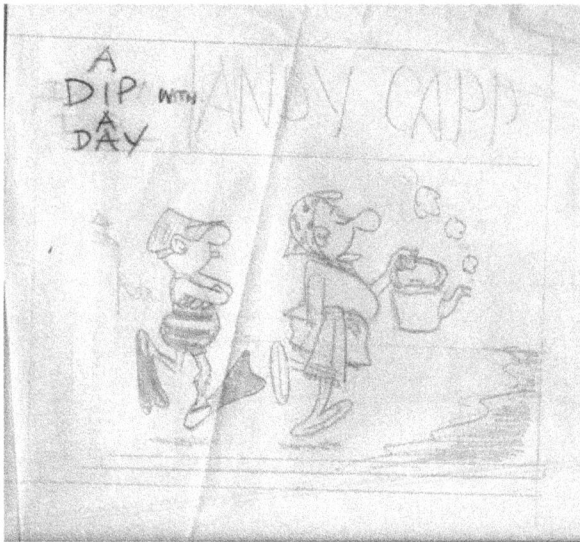

*Sketch working of Andy and Florrie from 70's —
both now shorter, rounder figures*

*Lily, Vera, Reg and myself on holiday in Antibes—
a favourite haunt of Reg.*

Multi panel cartoon replaced the single frame format by the '70s.

*Reg and Vera celebrating the first of his five
Cartoonist of the Year awards.*

Chapter 5

THE BOLSHY, WORKSHY little man in the black suit, flat cap and white muffler, with a half-smoked cigarette glued to his lip, was an enduring image of the swinging '60s. Andy Capp became as much a part of the cultural revolution as Mary Quant and The Beatles, taken up by intellectuals and middle class as well as the working class. Despite a way of life that appeared rooted in the '30s, Andy's irreverence captured a growing wave of anti-establishment feeling.

... I've often wondered why he appealed to younger people in the first few years. I think he served to confirm their prejudices about the older generation, although they admired his 'up yours' attitude. According to one critic he was a workingman's James Bond, in another a Crusader, but the one that tickled me the most was Malcolm Muggeridge's comparison with Woodhouse's butler, Jeeves. Both, he said, were dream figures, ageless and changeless ...

Reg was relishing the buzz of London; he and Vera rented a large flat in the centre of London's theatre land, aptly called

Grape Street, and with a bigger pay cheque were able to holiday abroad instead of the usual holiday camp. By now he had become an accepted if slightly envied figure in The Mirror studio, the first non-staff cartoonist to get a long-term contract and virtually a free hand from Hugh Cudlipp. Such was his popularity in the first few years of hitting the newspaper. Andy appeared in glorious isolation on Page 3 — traditionally given over to the political cartoons, and an event that Reg savoured as confirmation of having made it big time. However, he was at pains not to remove himself from the blokes in the studio.

... I still needed to feel part of a crowd; I worked hard at staying one of the boys but at the same time I deliberately cultivated a bit of a 'boyo' image which set me apart. They thought me slightly rakish, a bit of a dandy with my liking for bright waistcoats and Chelsea boots ... It gave them something to tease me about ... and confirmed my image of myself as set apart. I'd always felt like that — right from Grandmother's time ...

Reg's popularity with his peers, and his growing confidence as a cartoonist, put him in the thick of things, and was behind his decision to help found the Cartoonists Club of Great Britain in 1960. Along with agent Ian Scott, Reg was instrumental in getting it off the ground, and the inaugural meeting took place at a packed Fleet Street pub with more than 250 cartoonists. His work was rated highly among other cartoonists for both its professionalism and his unerring ability to make readers laugh — on a daily basis. That admiration went public when Reg was voted Cartoonist of the Year not once, but five times, the grinning gold and silver jester awards always given pride of place wherever he lived.

... Those award ceremonies were great times — nearly always at The Grosvenor or some other swanky London hotel, where you could get dressed up and feel that you had made it in your own 'community.' It changed though when I kept winning it — five times in all — and to tell the truth I started to feel embarrassed. I was glad

when the ceremony was disbanded. I guess I wanted the recognition without the attention...

Reg readily admitted the early drawings of Andy and Florrie were rather crude, with much of the strip gag-driven rather than character-led, as it was to become. The language, too, was broad and deliberately "Northern," with Reg dropping letters and using abbreviations like "yer," "owt" and "nowt" for effect. It was a measure of his standing that no sub-editor was allowed to change what in those days was a daring use of dialect.

... To begin with I drew how I had already drawn, Andy and Florrie looked like other characters I had created for the Laughter slot; they just dressed as I knew people did in the North of England. They were both thinner and taller, too, in the early drawings, which made them look younger – sort of in their 30s/early 40s was how I saw them. Their wardrobe reflected the younger, more aggressive edge which the cartoons had ...

However crude he thought the drawings, the strip had an avid following and by 1962 nine books of Andy cartoons had appeared, selling more than 850,000 copies each. He entered the public conscience to such an extent that the then prime minister, Harold Wilson, referred to "Mr Andy Capp not liking him putting up the price of beer" during a budget debate in the House of Parliament. Reg met Harold Wilson later when he was presented with his fifth "Oscar."

Life was sweet, but highly pressured, and the spaces in between visits back home grew longer. The subsequent void in Florrie's life led to a turbulent and destructive period, her quarrels with Percy grew more ferocious, and she used these as a reason to go out alone. Eventually she began disappearing for days as well as the odd weekend, coming back wearing new, loud clothes, their brashness matching her mood.

After months of hinting about an admirer, she admitted to Lily, who was now living back home, that she was seeing a 67-year-old widower called Fred. He was in trade, she said proudly, which in Florrie's eyes meant he was not only a desirable catch but had soft hands. As always, she had a nickname for him, "Creeping Jesus," which had nothing to do with his gait or his piety and everything to do with his sly, obsequious manner.

... There you go again ... if you mean smarmy say so ... that's what she whispered to me when she finally introduced us. It was the usual 'famous son' routine, although she made me feel like the prospective father in law. He was tall, which put me at a disadvantage, and sort of stooped, with a sweaty face and hands, which I thought suited his previous job as travelling salesman. Mother's version of being in trade ...

Like a latter-day Mata Hari, Florrie played Percy and Fred off against each other, moaning about one to the other as the villain of the hour. Her lurid tales of mistreatment resulted in several fights, which even she tried to end once she witnessed the two desperate old men rolling on the floor. But their jealousy was an intoxicating elixir, she felt young again and desired.

It was as if Andy and Florrie's fisticuffs, usually depicted in the cartoon by a large cloud of flying feet, was being played out on the kitchen floor in Hartlepool. Everyone was caught up in the hostilities, with Lily and Our Poor Jim either appeasing Florrie's mood swings or in separating the two combatants, who hissed threats like ageing gunslingers. Reg did make the occasional visit, but still unaware of Fred's existence, he was unable to explain the strained faces or uncomfortable atmosphere that hung around like stale breath.

Growing international success led to a tide of requests for interviews, and special material for books, while syndication, previously only done in a modest way, suddenly took off after Reg's cartoon was spotted in a Bermuda newspaper. It resulted in Reg becoming the first English cartoonist to break into the American market, and winning over a media notoriously hostile to any outsider.

When the chief of Hall Syndication first spotted Andy in a copy of Bermuda's The Advocate the cartoon was already syndicated to 28 countries. Despite his description of Andy to his colleagues as a "bully and a limey," they immediately got in touch with The Daily Mirror to secure syndication rights for the U.S. market. And their faith was rewarded, in a single month syndication climbed to over 90 papers, from the Washington Post and Chicago Tribune to Louis Post-Dispatch and the Iowa Times Republican. By the second year the cartoon was appearing in 400 papers.

Al Capp, the revered American creator of Li'l Abner was an immediate fan, telegraphing Reg: "You've broken all the rules. None of us back home would have ventured to hand the public a husband who is both a drunk and a lecher – but since you came on the scene we're all in danger of being out of date."

The American success led to a change of format from the single panel cartoon to a more flexible comic-book layout, four frames which initially were in a square formation before becoming the horizontal strip it now is. Reg sometimes had to draw extra frames for the USA, but believed this extra "padding" as he called it took away from the cartoons precision and punch. It was heady times, but also caused Reg's ulcer to start playing up once again.

... I think that might have subconsciously been why Vera and I started to take longer and longer breaks to the South of France. We had already been on a holiday, driving down in my small MG, and I felt more free than I had done since those early days in the army. We became friends with a wonderful, PG Woodhouse kind of guy called Steve who had stayed on after the war and owned a cafe in Juan-Les-Pins. He and his wife Renee allowed us to rent their flat and suddenly a couple of weeks became three months, which was how it continued for a few years ... although I still felt like an outsider looking in, I had a nickname for myself then – the little Gatsby ...

Reg told me how on their first night in the fashionable French resort, he had suddenly burst out laughing. When

Vera asked what was wrong, he replied that he had just imagined Andy sitting with them at the restaurant, sending back the steak tartar and frits for some "proper" food. The contrasts with life back in Hartlepool seemed to reinforce how far he'd come, and suddenly Hartlepool, Florrie and all her intrigues no longer seemed important. Reg certainly enjoyed the irony of his new situation.

... I didn't stop drawing, of course. I just changed the venue. I took my own little board and a stack of card and paper with me to the South of France so I could do it anywhere. ... And we got our routine quickly in place, drawing all morning on the terrace – the usual storylines, Andy going down the boozer or the pool hall. Then I'd go down to one of the wonderful manicured beaches and swim. It felt glorious, it also felt safe. I think I began to feel I had finally made the break from mother, and from all those feelings of shame and guilt which went with her ... Amazingly, The Mirror accepted the situation, no quibbles as long as I went back for a few days each month to deliver the batch of cartoons ...

I remember joining them, with my mother, for a week's holiday, driving down in his gleaming green Mercedes to Lyon and then on the train to Nice. Reg loved trains; his favourite game was playing characters from films, like Hitchcock's "The 39 Steps," encouraging us to creep along railway corridors and act suspiciously in front of the uncomprehending French train guard. It was the same sense of childish fun which Florrie had, and which he could not acknowledge.

It might have been the South of France, but Reg's interests remained the same; he continued to enjoy gambling, swapping the betting shop for a Cannes casino, and exchanging a familiar drinking haunt for a busy bar called The Pam Pam, where the Scottish owner was an Andy fan, and always found Reg and Vera a quiet corner to watch the never-ending parade of beautiful people bent on pleasure.

In the intervening months in London, Reg steadily grew thinner and thinner, and during one of his weekends back in

Hartlepool his ulcer flared up so badly he had to be stretchered back to London in an ambulance. He had an emergency operation for a duodenal ulcer and part of his stomach removed; for the first time in his life, Reg got to eat an orange. At the same time Florrie got to own her first ever house.

She had persuaded Fred that the only thing keeping them apart was Percy and having to live in his house; Fred used some of his considerable savings to buy her a terraced house in West Hartlepool, little realising that she was envisaging a ménage à trois. She couldn't just abandon Percy, she explained, he could live in the attic. As it turned out, Fred got to be the lodger and eventually, fed up with this arrangement and the realisation that Florrie was no more his than before, disappeared.

During the long convalescence, Reg began drawing extra cartoons in case he was ill again, building up a considerable store. He was now approaching the peak of his success, and in the heady years which followed he was also to face something he had not faced before—criticism, and not only from the rising feminist voice in the U.S. but from people in England, too. It forced him to look afresh at what he had created.

Chapter 6

THE TROUBLE with success is there are fewer windmills to tilt against, and Reg still liked to think of himself as a rebel. The cartoon's anti-hero popularity helped reinforced this self-image, and he worked hard to maintain a sharp, uncompromising edge to its humour.

Readers continued to love him, despite or because of his being a "work-shy, beer-swilling, rent-dodging, pigeon-fancier, skirt-chasing, soccer-playing uncouth cadger." Andy became synonymous with a particular type of behaviour and lifestyle, like Don Juan or Mussolini. And yet the uniqueness of the cartoon came from Andy or Florrie behaving the opposite way to what was expected. The cartoon could deliver a perfect punch line, or gag, but the added element of surprise, usually in the last frame, where the character demands the readers' collusion made the cartoon unique.

One of Reg's own favourites was Andy down at the police station saying he wants a word with the bloke arrested for breaking into his house. "Now then, lad," says the police sergeant, "we don't like folk taking the law into their own hands." Andy looks hurt, and replies, "I just wanted to know how he got in without waking the missus, that's all." Another favourite had Florrie addressing the reader while Andy is trying to convince her that going to the pub means they can save on heating, lighting, TV and the gas. Arms folded, she looks out at the reader and says, "Anytime now he'll convince me that we'll be showing a profit."

... He's a devil isn't he? That's what I like people to think of him, almost with affection. It's a persona I cultivate, too, both with women and men. That kind of banter only works between childless couples. Somehow the roles get mixed up and one or the other plays the child ... it's a sort of pantomime that married people the world over recognise. That technique of talking straight at the reader is akin to film writing, something which has always fascinated me, perhaps that's where I got the original idea, I don't know ...

At the height of his success Andy was ranked alongside other cartoon greats like Peanuts and Garfield. In one year he even knocked American's long time favourite, Blondie, into third place. And the creator of Li'l Abner hailed Reg as the most popular English humourist since Charles Dickens. But whereas the success of Charles Schulz's Peanuts and Jim Davis's Garfield was a clever mix of merchandising and drawing, Reg's success was largely down to the cartoon alone.

The Mirror's then Managing Editor Hugh Cudlipp was anti- anything to do with merchandising, afraid too much exposure would kill the strip's popularity. He was first and foremost a newspaper man, and circulation was his god.

... Mind you, who'd want a T-shirt with Andy on when you can have a cute cat or dog. Better still, cute boy with cute dog. It all changed after Cudlipp ...

It was as if Andy touched a common nerve in every society; in the 1,500 or so newspapers which took the cartoon nothing was changed, only the name—Tufa Viktor, Kasket Karl, Willie Wacker, Angello Capello, Linke Loetje and Zé do

Boné to name a few. All claimed him as their own; an editor from Istanbul wrote: *"Andy must be a Turkish fellow, he looks and behaves typically like us."*

There was enormous curiosity about the cartoon and its creator, BBC North produced "The World of Andy Capp" while Granada Television devoted its "People and Places" programme to the cartoon. Reg was reluctantly driven back to the North East by the producer to film the fast disappearing terrace streets and local pubs. Filming took place in the Manchester studios, and it was to begin a love affair with the City, which remained with him for the rest of his life. It was also where he and Jean managed to spend time alone together in their Manchester flat, savouring the club life.

... There was something vibrant about Manchester throughout the '60s and early '70s ... no discos, just piano bars and supper clubs all featuring heroes of mine like Tommy Cooper and Dave Allen. ... many of whom I met ... amazingly I never felt awkward with them. I would usually send a little card with a drawing of Andy, and invite them over for a drink after the show ... the intimacy of the clubs, and perhaps the brandy, helped with any shyness, we were just two blokes, doing what we were good at, swapping life stories ...

And Reg needed the rawness of Manchester once he and Vera had to leave their beloved West End London flat. With property in central London hard to find, they were forced further out of London, and eventually bought a small detached house in Harrow. For the first time he felt unable to draw from home. He did not find any inspiration in the leafy suburbs, and a couple of times each week he joined the hundreds of commuters to go up to the Mirror studios. But that too was changing, with the Mirror's cartoon studio now hived off from Fleet Street.

... What was the point of working in London if I couldn't live there? The whole point was being in the thick of it, the drinking clubs, the atmosphere ... I could choose to take part, or not. But stuck out in the suburbs there was no choice. I would stare out at blokes washing their cars on Sunday with real distaste ...

He needed the fix of visiting Hartlepool even more, which now included sister Lily and me on the impromptu journeys North. We had decamped to the capital after a falling out with Florrie over Fred's, *"Creeping Jesus"* habit of writing anonymous letters against people he imagined were keeping Florrie from him; I was one of them. One of his efforts landed on my headmistress's desk, its sensational accusations about my out-of-school activities at odds with the overweight, clumsy girl who stood before her. For Lily it was the last straw. I left school on the next Friday, and on the Monday my mother and I were in London. In one day we both found jobs and somewhere to live.

The visits North were the usual mix of warm welcome and spiky flare-ups; Florrie was taking to advancing age very badly, refusing to accept Percy's growing frailty as an excuse for not going out, looking to Reg to provide the social diversions. Despite changes to the town, there were still the old, familiar pubs to visit, and the North Eastern was one of his favourites, swapping jokes with Landlord Jackie and barmaid Madge.

In 1975 Reg was awarded the U.S. equivalent of the cartoon "Oscar," the National Cartoonists Society's Best Strip of the Year Award, and flew over to collect the award. Walking down Broadway, through Central Park and Manhattan were remembered highlights, he was seeing the New York he knew from a thousand films. Later he said he preferred the celluloid, but Reg's imagination was always richer than anything real life could offer.

So much exposure resulted in other reactions, not always favourable. A backlash developed from a vocal minority against this idle, boozy little man. How come he never worked? Why did he have to bash Florrie about so much? Andy came to epitomise in many eyes what was wrong with certain sectors of society, and the North in particular.

Even in pre-Thatcher's Britain he began to be regarded by some as an anachronism, out of step with the escalating entrepreneurial fever. But he dealt with most of the criticism in typical gentle, humorous style, refusing to get into any debates about the political correctness of it all.

When asked why Andy had no drive, no ambition, he replied that of course he did. It took commitment and ingenuity to stay unemployed for as long as Andy had.

Reg's response to telephone interviews became increasingly defensive; when asked why he never introduced children into the cartoon he replied it would be obscene to have Andy stealing money from Florrie's purse if they had kids. It just wasn't right, he said.

... When people wrote asking how he could afford cigarettes and booze on the welfare, I replied that knowing Andy he had probably raffled his dole money. That was an answer which I felt was in keeping with the character. What the 'knockers' did do though, and I am eternally grateful, is get me to think long and hard about what I thought about the cartoon. I realised that all the boozing and not working were side shows really, the core of the cartoon for me was the man, woman thing ... an unequal relationship maybe, but never static. Sometimes Andy won, sometimes Florrie got one over on him. The wife-bashing threw it out of balance somehow, concentrating too much attention on one area – his brutality I suppose, and not on the play between the two of them ...

Slowly the fisticuffs between the two were phased out, although Florrie was still regularly seen with arms folded, rolling pin in hand ready to ladle it out to Andy for some misdemeanour. Florrie's mistreatment continued, but was now shown through Andy's often callous attitude, like the cartoon where Florrie dashes in from the fish and chip shop saying she's been chased all the way by a strange man. Good, says Andy, the chips will be hot for a change.

It marked the onset of middle-age for the Capps, and a change in drawing style. Andy became more cuddlier somehow, a little shorter than Florrie, who was drawn more buxom and maternal, to emphasise what Reg now saw as the key to the whole cartoon, the mother/boy relationship that had developed between the two of them.

That was what Reg encouraged, too, allowing all the women in his life to take care of him, and not expecting him to become overly involved in domestic activities, which gave him permission to draw uninterrupted. Bits of his own philosophy frequently crept into the cartoon, for instance he has Andy advising a young bridegroom at the wedding reception, "always look a little bit hurt, son. That keeps them on their toes." Reg's variation, which he joked about, but which he employed to great effect echoed his mother's advice, "to always look a bit disappointed." He put into words an attitude that his mother Florrie had naturally adopted with admirers over the years; she gave the impression they could never please her enough, but if they could, they would win her total love and approval. For them it was akin to the Holy Grail.

Changes to Andy and Florrie were not the only development; Reg became increasingly economic with other characters too. Superfluous characters were dropped, other than the small repertory of players like next-door neighbours Chalkie and Rube, Jackie the publican and Percy the rent man. Drawings became more stylised, the first years saw Andy drawn from all angles and in countless settings, from Blackpool holidays to hospital beds, now it was limited largely to the house, the pub or the playing field, all shown flat on and presented through medium and short range angles.

The avoidance of long distance shots was just one of the effects Reg employed to bring the reader into Andy's world and make them involved. A French student who chose to study Andy for her MA described this effect in her thesis as an "Italian shot."

... Can you imagine that? Apparently this is where a character is drawn just to his knees, or just to the waistline. One of my own favourite techniques was the out of sight shot, where the action takes

place outside the frame, but I show what the characters say in a speech balloon, and it gives the gag much more emphasis. An example would be one I had three frames showing a conversation between Andy and Flo either side of the front door. He's begging to be taken back, saying he's hungry. She asks him if he likes cold chicken; he replied he wouldn't eat it any other way. Final frame sees Andy, in the rain, sitting on his suitcase, looking fed up, as he hears her voice from the other side says, 'fine, come back tomorrow. The chicken is hot right now.' ... That French student reckoned I did that out of sight technique to underline how much of an outsider Andy was from society ... sounds a bit grand to me, I don't like to think too deeply, otherwise it becomes too precious ... I hope she got her MA though ...

The idea to return to Hartlepool to live was not something that happened suddenly, it gradually evolved over a few months, perhaps even a year he had told me. Living in Harrow was becoming increasingly frustrating, it was hard persuading cabs to make the journey out of London, so Reg endured travelling on the tube. Even trips to the Mirror were not as enjoyable as they once were, there was less time to socialise with the Studio team and more demands for meetings and extra cartoons for merchandising, which had now taken a firm grip. Andy appeared on beer mugs and tea towels, and was asked to endorse everything from drinking chocolate to saving bonds.

This growing frustration coincided with enjoyable weekends in Hartlepool, where Florrie was on her best behaviour. She was good company, anxious to spoil her visitors and great fun. The sauce bottles were new, the Yorkshire puddings done to perfection and the bacon just how he liked it. Hartlepool looked inviting in the spring sunshine; he would drive over to the headland, the oldest part of the town with its solitary pier and angry waves, recalling youthful memories and a girl called Esther who liked to watch Pierrot shows on the sea front.

Reg was now 59, he had lived in London for nearly 30 years and Andy had been one of the nation's favourite cartoons for 20 years. He had been the first to break into the lucrative American syndication market and had won just about every cartoon award possible. But it was Andy who people identified with, not Reg Smythe and suddenly he found he minded. It was the first time I heard him refer to Andy as his dancing bear. This was a reference to singer/songwriter Alan Price's hit song Simon Smith and His Amazing Dancing Bear, with the lyrics, "who would guess a boy and bear could be well accepted anywhere; it's just amazing how fair people can be ... "

... I remember there had been some quiz show on TV and contestants were asked to name three top cartoonists, they replied Terence 'Larry' Parkes, Carl Giles and Andy Capp. I wasn't even mentioned, I hadn't entered the public conscious the way he had. Although that anonymity was what I wanted, I was surprised to now feel left out ... But I did. Back in Hartlepool I was on a level with him. I was Reggie Smythe, who drew Andy Capp. That wasn't the main reason for going back home though, it was as much to do with avoiding the rush hour as any other ... and hating the suburbs ...

One day he came out with what he had been thinking about for some time, let's move back up North, he announced. Vera, who would be closer to her family in Hull, readily agreed; Jean, too, saw no reason to stay in London without him. The Daily Mirror saw no problems either, Reg had always drawn from home, he would make trips a couple of times a month to bring his cartoons down, that's all.

Florrie was most delighted, except when he told her that he was working and would probably have much less time for going out than he had before. But she cheered up when Lily announced she was also returning home. London without Reg was unimaginable for all of them.

So in April 1976, Reg and Vera drew up outside their new bungalow to find a barrage of reporters and television cameras waiting on the pavement outside. Reg was surprisingly patient and co-operative with each journalist who wanted their own slant on the story. "Andy comes home," "Return of the Native" were the sort of newspaper headlines, with the local press keen to play up the North / South divide, suggesting it might have been southern hospitality which drove him north. It was a suggestion Reg was quick to refute.

... People up North are fundamentally no better or worse than in the south. Put a Hartlepudlian in London and he'll soon start behaving like a Londoner ... I lived there for nearly 30 years, so I must have loved it, and I did to start with, although deep down I still thought of myself as a Northern lad — that's how I was perceived anyway — and yet now I'm up here I feel more southern, a bit 'soft' ...

The initial furore soon died down and Reg quickly got into his usual rhythm of drawing five days a week, taking off Mondays and Fridays to deal with correspondence and fan mail. But if anyone thought he would take more time off they were wrong, for Reg free time meant time-wasting, it had to be an inviting film or get together to get him to stop drawing. An exception was the Boilermaker's Club, one of those working men clubs which are a feature of the North of England, and where the crack, or conversation, and sometimes cruel male banter reassured him that Andy Capp was alive and well.

Reg was kept busy in the first year or two of returning to Hartlepool, although he still turned down the majority of interviews, there were frequent requests for comments about local events and extra material for the region's press or charities. He also found he could enjoy London again, the short journeys once a month to deliver cartoons allowed him to keep up with gossip at The Mirror, have lunch at a favourite restaurant, and wander around familiar haunts. Life seemed to be slowing down, both for him and Andy, except something happened which flung both of them onto the centre stage — but not before Florrie's death.

Chapter 7

FLORRIE WAS 79 when Reg moved back to Hartlepool, for the first time she was living without a man, but being Florrie, that did not mean living alone. Percy had died a few years before, and she had since gathered an odd assembly of characters around her. Reg called them "the botched and the bungled," a line from a favourite film.

They were needy, child-like people who saw in her open door and ready warmth a haven from a more judgemental world. Florrie was still bright and alert, physically smaller but in the right light, and with the right makeup, capable of appearing at least ten years younger than she was. Personality-wise, she was 19; she still enjoyed a bottle of brown ale, or two, still played the horses and still saw money as the means for winning friends and having a good time. Above all, she could not bear to be alone.

Florrie's followers included Maggie, with her expanding brood of children, David, a gentle lame boy, and Evelyn who, along with her less opportunistic sister, ran a lonely hearts club offering romance to sailors on far-flung ships. Reg's comment was that if they had seen Evelyn, or any of her lonely hearts, the sailors would stay far-flung. Florrie's little house was nearly always full of people, most of them waifs and strays, and, although they stayed away when the more straight-laced Lily first came home, they slowly resumed visiting rights.

Reg had already met most of this odd assortment on previous visits, and admitted to feeling awkward around their wordless admiration. When Charlie and Percy were alive there could be a pretence of normality, now there was none. He visited her less, using the excuse of settling in or pressures of work, the excuses gradually drying up, but by then Reg and Florrie had had a major disagreement. For the first time he allowed his unspoken hostility towards her to break out into the open, and they stopped speaking until a few months before her death.

... She seemed out of control. Her liking to play everyone off against the other was pointless and irritating. I was now living in the town, so was my sister, everything she always said she wanted. But that wasn't enough ... she had a voracious need for something — I don't know what. Perhaps that's why she decided to get married again, but the stupidity of it seemed to be a deliberate attempt at humiliating me. The local press loved it, women's page editors writing how love transcends the age barrier guff. She was quoted as saying 'I've known him since he was a little boy.' Christ, she sounded like a child molester ... I was livid ...

Florrie's third husband was John, a 47-year-old man with a square cut jaw and a drunk's appetite for words, regarded by the local police as too insignificant to be even a petty criminal. Egged on by the Lonely Hearts, who saw romance in all the wrong places, Florrie encouraged his attentions.

She hated living alone; Reg's visits were fewer and not so exciting as his sudden dashes from London, even the put-upon Lily had found somewhere else to live. On the spur of the moment, Florrie agreed to marry him. The local press had a field day; the first Reg heard was a call from the local paper asking him what he thought of his new stepfather. Grotesque, he replied.

His comments, and the reality of living with John, forced a sober new realisation upon Florrie. There was a half-hearted suicide attempt; I visited her in hospital and she asked me to bring her make-up in. "I never meant it, you know pet," I thought she meant the marriage to John, but she was talking about leaving Reg's father.

A divorce was speedily arranged and Lily moved back home to live with her. But Florrie was no longer the same; in growing up, Florrie had grown old. In a final act of atonement she signed the house over to Lily, who, like her mother, had never owned property. She began to mix with ladies her age and smile that sweet, half-vacant smile of the very old.

Florrie contracted stomach cancer in 1982, and while in hospital Reg came to see her. He was dreading histrionics, but she was restrained, almost regal, which in itself was oddly moving. She died in September, and at the funeral, which was a noisy, jolly affair, we learnt of a different Florrie. Distant relatives spoke of a younger, softer woman who would turn up on her sisters' doorsteps with black eyes or bruised face. We did not want to remember her that way, Reg particularly so.

... Who was this vulnerable girl they talked about? I certainly didn't recognise her, it was always Florrie who dished it out. Even her death seemed unreal, I was so involved in her world and in drawing it every day, she was still here. I refused to feel pity or regret when I saw her in hospital – for some reason I kept hearing Grandmother Smyth saying "actress" ... for so long she was the bastard, she had to stay that way – to think otherwise would be unbearable ...

The year Florrie died saw moves to bring Andy Capp to the stage; it had been half-heartedly mooted before, but Reg had been decidedly ambivalent. Andy's world was so tightly drawn he was not confident it would translate to a larger stage. But others thought differently, and, as he signed away the copyright of Andy Capp long ago, he could do little than go along with the producers' enthusiasm.

However, he couldn't have had a better team working on a musical than Alan Price, an established singer songwriter with a similar background to Reg, and writer and actor Trevor Peacock as his collaborator, who had already written four other musicals. It was a good team with a proven creative record, but Andy was no easy format.

... I was invited to act as a consultant to the show, but in truth that mattered little, other than a look at the final script. The writers used my books for background or if they were beaten for a gag, that's all. Their picture of Andy was different from mine. I only remember once demurring with the director when he had Andy use a four-letter word. I said that would never happen, men from his background never swore outside their tight, all-male enclave. It sent him into hysterics ... but then creators are never happy, are they?

Peacock's method of developing what was essentially a character-led gag into a two hour show was to plaster as many cartoons as he could all over his office to try and get at the heart of the strip. His conclusion was the same as Reg—that it was to do with the eternal battle between the sexes, "His life was locked into hers, and hers to his" he was quoted as saying. But that was just the start.

Whereas other musicals based on cartoons had an unfolding storyline, Andy was different. There was no real story, simply the characters combined with first-rate gags, so he created a plot around a young couple, distantly related to the Capps, who are getting married. Conflict arises from the clash between the bride and groom's families, with the bride's mother dominating the hen-pecked dad and the groom's lot being more like Andy. The show's highlight was when the bride's father takes his savings to the pub, announcing, "I just want to say bollocks to my wife and secondly, the drinks are on me." Reg's view was that Andy would have been appalled, both by the language and the idea of paying for drinks. But it brought the house down.

The casting for Andy Capp was always going to be controversial; he was eventually played by Tom Courtenay, a respected English actor better known for his classical roles that had a previous musical connection with Trevor Peacock. Physically, of course, he was very different, taller and thinner, but perhaps most disconcerting as far as Andy fans were concerned, the cap was off, and Tom's face revealed.

... It was difficult for Tom, having to create someone that everyone thought they knew from 30 years of imagining what his face and expressions were like – his interpretation was bound to be at odds with theirs ... Other people don't see Andy as I see him. I imagine him as a belligerent but a naturally perky, upbeat sort of bloke. In the musical he came across as a bit flat-footed ...

The show opened at the Royal Exchange in Manchester before transferring to the Aldwych in London's West End, where it ran for six or seven months. Reviews were mixed and generally lukewarm. Reg went to see it several times, and again when it was produced by The Tyne Theatre Company at The Newcastle Playhouse. This time, the North Eastern actor Tim Healey played Andy Capp and Reg felt happier with his interpretation, feeling he wasn't afraid to show up Andy's nastiness, or what he preferred to call, his naughty side.

With Florrie gone, Reg appeared to withdraw slightly further into his own imagination. He still enjoyed outings to The Boilermaker's Club, and summer holidays on the South Coast, where he and Vera had bought a flat; his memories and inventiveness provided all he needed to recreate Andy's world. He knew it so well that he only had to look at a situation or a boy passing by on roller blades to know instinctively how Andy would react. With the popularity of the cartoon assured, and the fan mail coming in, The Daily Mirror were happy to renew his contract for another seven years. He was now 66.

Andy's antics could still make front-page news, as was shown with press reaction to the news that both Reg and Andy had stopped smoking. One heavyweight newspaper wrote solemnly, "One of the great icons of British cartoon art has quietly given up the half-smoked cigarette which has dangled from his lower lip for 26 years." The anti-smoking lobby were delighted, particularly when Reg was quoted as saying it was time to set a good example; too many children read the cartoon. The more likely explanation was Reg's identification with the character was so complete that he couldn't imagine Andy smoking without him.

Five years after the musical, there was another attempt to bring Andy Capp off the page, this time by one-time head of BBC Comedy, Jim Gilbert, who had switched to Thames TV and was looking for comedy ideas. The leading role was quickly decided, going to well known actor James Bolam, who not only came from the North East, but had starred in the nation's favourite comedy about two Northern boys, The Likely Lads. The consensus among many was that, while not physically like Andy, Bolam was ideal for the role.

International publisher Robert Maxwell had now taken over the Mirror Group, and had thrown his considerable weight behind the concept of a television series; he stated he was very fond of the strip and much to Reg's dread he invited him for lunch next time he was in London.

... I was not looking forward to it ... I needn't have worried, he did all the talking, throwing his huge, bear-like arm around my shoulders as we ploughed up and down his office. Andy, he boomed, was the jewel in the Mirror's crown. I should have known better, we went for lunch and he let me pay. He was so like my brother-in-law, Eddy, that I couldn't help but like him. He had the same continental charm, the same absolute confidence in everything and then letting you down in the end ... but everyone was mesmerised, just like with Eddy all those years before ...

Keith Waterhouse, a Daily Mirror columnist and successful author, was asked to write the series. The writer and director were faced with similar dilemmas to the musical producers, how to turn a cartoon strip into something sustainable for 30 minutes. Keith Waterhouse decided early on to retain the cartoon essence by having characters speak directly to the viewers, he also developed a specific theme for each of the six episodes.

The director, John Howard Davies, similarly wanted to retain as much as possible of the cartoon flavour, daringly opting for filming rather than recording in the studio before an audience. There was a stylised look the show, with Davies using a still camera so that characters fell in and out of "frames"; he remained further true to the cartoon by recreating set pieces, such as the back shot of Andy and Chalkie at the bar, Andy on the sofa, glass outstretched for Florrie to fill, and making sure Andy's mother-in-law stayed strictly off camera.

There was a lot going for it, so why then did it not achieve the ratings many thought it deserved? Opinions vary, but the lack of audience laughter and a ridiculously early scheduling were factors. Others believed, Reg among them, that the essential character of Andy had somehow been diluted.

... It's hard to imagine anyone wanting to spend more than a few minutes with such a basically obnoxious bloke, to do so you had to either make him more loveable or take him down a peg or two – neither works. It's okay to spend a few seconds chuckling each morning, quite another thing to be asked to spend longer in his company ... and that's the dilemma. Although that was achieved very successfully some years later on TV with Ian Pattison's Glasgow horror Rab C. Nesbitt. He managed to be both revolting, a drunk, a loser and yet retain his humanity. Now there's someone Andy would love to drink with ...

While Reg was disappointed with both the musical and television series, he never felt responsible for either, because he had not been directly involved. Their Andy was not his. He knew his character inside out, and his day-to-day relationship with him remained unchanged. Reg detached himself, emotionally as well as physically from both productions, pragmatically summing up how he felt in a letter to a fan in the States:

... I wasn't involved in either the musical or television series, which is as it should be, they are completely different mediums from mine. And, as you know, the creator is never happy. I always console myself with the thought that if the programme is good, there'll be some personal praise, and if it isn't so good, then people will go on about it not being anywhere near as satisfying as the newspaper strip ...

Slowly Reg's links with the past were disappearing, sister Lily died in 1987, and his brother, "Our Poor Jimmy," had died many years earlier. One link remained, Nellie Smyth, who was the widow of his father's younger brother, Tom. Here was someone who remembered his Smyth childhood and knew all the stories about Florrie. Over 90, and as ladylike and frail as Florrie had been down to earth and tough, Nellie delighted in his letters and he readily encouraged her still vivid memories during his visits to her home in North Yorkshire.

The drawing continued to be a source of pleasure and commitment, rain or shine saw him in the den, drawing and searching for ideas. He had now begun to lengthen his days, often drawing late into the night and early morning. He would take a few hours off at night to watch a programme, but then, if an idea came or something sparked his imagination, he would jot something down in an exercise book in his clear, copperplate handwriting. Mostly, he liked to get ahead of himself, as he explained, pencilling in the figures ready to be inked in the next day. It was as if Reg still drew to a timetable, like when he first used an alarm clock to make sure he stuck to 30 minutes per cartoon.

His drawings were now pared down to the essential characters, he instinctively knew the right spacing of dialogue across the frames, while the signature off-stage comments and eyeballing the reader were all masterfully done. Although first printed in colour in the early '70s, Reg continued to pen the cartoons in black and white, which reinforced their stark reality. He still used the small white china pot he had used for years to paint in the blue washes to denote shadows, everything was as it had always been, except the determination to maintain standards was more fixed than ever. However sweet life was, he never took his success for granted.

... Sometimes on early taxi rides to the station, on my way to London and The Mirror, I would pass blokes in the early light waiting for lifts, shifting from foot to foot in the morning frost, queuing for the first bus. I always felt lucky, poor buggers I thought, that could be me ...

Reg also knew exactly what Andy had done for him; he sometimes talked as though the character was a real entity, something apart from himself rather than his creation. A favourite quote with interviewers, was that he knew Andy could be a devil, but he'd been very good to him. How good, was apparent in the last year of Reg's life.

Lily getting out of Reg's much loved green Mercedes, pride of place outside Florrie's house.

*Reg, inking in a drawing on his knee –
his daily, never-ending routine.*

The now familiar strip cartoon format.

Reg giving prizes at the "Andy Capp Handicap" horse race in Redcar.

Rare shot of Reg in garden — still drawing!

*Reg backstage at the "Andy Capp Musical" (1986)
with Tom Courtenay, Alan Price and cast.*

A publicity shot by Daily Mirror 1992.

*Jean, Reg's second wife, unveiling the
bronze statue of Andy in 2011.*

Chapter 8

WHEN REG said, or even wrote, the word "Mother," it always sounded like an insult, with a swallowing of the vowels so the word sounded clipped and unnatural. After she died he rarely used the word again, if he talked about Florrie, it was always her or she. Yet, through the cartoons she remained as real and alive as ever. Her physical shape resembled Florrie's matronly curves, but it was through Andy Capp and their shared characteristics of childish cunning and selfishness that Florrie could be glimpsed.

Andy continued to drag him into the wider world whenever possible, such as Robert Maxwell's insistence that Andy spearhead the publicity campaign for The Mirror's share flotation in 1991. This included full-page colour advertisements and an animated Andy featured in television commercials. All of which made Reg uneasy, he knew that greater exposure could lead to a renewal of criticism. He was right, with some newspapers airing the strip's more contentious history, like the earlier domestic violence. Reg was weary of the debate; it was left to other Mirror columnists to defend him, such as an imagined letter by Florrie to agony aunt Marje Proops.

... I just wanted the whole thing forgotten ... instead we had this sentimental tosh written by 'Florrie,' admitting that Andy used to knock her about a bit but now she'd tamed him ... he's a reformed character, she said, he wouldn't swat a fly. They were trying to sanitise him and it was killing the character ... I'd dropped it because I started to become fed up with defending what was pretty indefensible, but that didn't mean it didn't happen. It was also part of a character like him ... he wouldn't stop because it was morally wrong, he would have just got older ... and ran out of puff ...

Whatever Andy did made news. The New York Times picked up on a story, which implied Andy Capp was going to take off his cap as part of a Council's campaign to change outworn perceptions of Northern England. The public reaction, and Reg's, too, at any attempt to clean up Andy's image was immediate and hostile. He knew that the cartoon's success had to do with readers relating directly to Andy, they really knew what made him tick and it was from this recognition of the character, not the situation, that the humour sprang.

Like before, the outrage died down and Reg was left to get on with what he did best. He was now the grand old man of cartooning, admired as much for staying at the top for so long as the cartoon itself. His work was held up by tutors to students, who were advised to study the accurate layouts, the visual symmetry of the characters, and how each frame complemented the other. Reg's advice to budding cartoonists was invariably the same, please the cartoon editor first with what he thinks his readers want, and try to work in a domestic theme because that always worked. Cartooning, he would tell students, was a job and not an art form. Many fans of his work thought differently.

Syndication continued to be popular, with the strip winning new readers. Reg had stopped wondering about Andy's worldwide appeal; the explanation he liked best was that of Richard Hoggart, a respected English professor and literary critic, who attributed the cartoon's success to flattering men in a society where they are not as powerful as they would like to be, and flatters women because it convinces them they really do wear the trousers.

When asked what came first, the idea or the drawing, Reg would reply that the words and drawing were both vital, but it was the idea, which was the starting point. You could just about have a good gag with a lousy drawing, but not the other way round. By now, Reg had plenty of time to know what worked and didn't, and he continued to think about his work and refine it, if possible. He worried at one point that the cartoon suffered from being too wordy, and tried hard to ensure he was as brief and to the point as much as possible. I remember him explaining how he applied the "fresh fish" test before finishing an outline:

... *Most cartoons benefit from a caption, but put too many words in and it kills both the joke and drawing. Andy is sometimes a little more gabby than I like, but by the time I send the cartoons off they are as brief as I can get them ... If I'm unsure I use the 'fresh fish sold here' test ... the fishmonger takes out 'sold' because customers know he's not giving it away, then he takes out 'fresh' because it implies his fish aren't, then he omits 'here' because if anyone is reading the sign it means they have found him ... That leaves 'Fish.' Simple and to the point ...*

Reg's work was now conducted by telephone and post; he finally stopped going to London altogether, preferring instead to use a private courier service to deliver his neat, monthly parcels of cartoons to The Mirror offices in East London. He explained it gave him more time to draw which was mostly true, it took considerable energy to come up with five or six cartoons a day, and also to keep up the stock for "emergencies," he was determined not to let his output slip.

Reg's memories and imagination were now the sole wellspring for the Andy material; The Boilermaker's Club had closed down, and places he remembered were disappearing in the town's drive to modernise itself. Events while on holiday, or on television would occasionally inspire him, particularly the more outrageous chat shows which got him thinking how Andy would react, but more often than not he turned to his earlier work.

... I am not ashamed of reusing old material and giving it a new slant – I don't think a cartoonist's job is to be original, my job is to be sharp and funny ... a good gag is always worth retelling, as long as it's given a slightly updated look. When I first thought up the idea, I would have probably written a few different versions anyway – and I never threw anything away ...

Like Florrie, Reg never considered himself old or even getting older. He enjoyed wearing bright, fashionable clothes and, like her, he had an unerring knack of always looking good. Drawing Andy bestowed a kind of immortality, it was as if he had found his own fountain of youth. I realised he existed in a time capsule of his own making, which had something to do with the cartoon's 1950s origins, but more to do with the timelessness of the character he created. Andy was essentially a fantasy character, who could behave as badly as he liked, for as long as he liked, without hurting anyone. Perhaps Reg had the best of both creative worlds, he could both live in the past, while his inner world created this timeless fantasy world. Any interruption to this quiet, addictive inner life was unwelcome.

Vera's sudden death in 1997 punctured that time capsule. Her routine was as fixed as Reg's, with set days for outings and set times for doing things. Vera was dressed and made up, ready for her regular shopping trip, when she suffered a massive heart attack one May morning.

Her death was a tremendous shock, she had not complained of any illness and, like Reg, enjoyed defying the ageing process. She was my greatest fan, he would say; she had believed in him from the beginning, and then simply stood back as the character he created took centre stage. It was to her credit that she combined looking after him while tolerating, if not accepting, his other life with Jean.

Andy came to Reg's rescue in the first few months following her death, the self-imposed need to keep up the daily schedule meant he could escape from people and also immerse himself in something other than what had happened. And in order to maintain that safe, closed routine he turned to Jean, who knew that world intimately, and who always hoped they could be together openly one day.

... I've always liked being looked after, even in the army ... and I've been lucky in that there has always been someone to do that ... I know that makes me sound like Andy, and I know there's bits of him in me, I think there is in most men. But sometimes I'd play that up a bit, like when reporters would visit I would deliberately turn a cup of tea Vee had just brought me, and ask her if she had forgotten something. She would say sorry darling, bring back some sugar and turn the tea cup handle towards me ... it was a kind of in joke, one of those running jokes which married people have ...

The same year Vera died, an exhibition entitled Forty Years of Andy Capp, organised by the University of Kent's Centre for The Study of Cartoons and Caricature began its countrywide tour. When it came to Hartlepool Reg did not go to see it, he was too busy drawing he said, but part of him felt Andy was too much alive for such a retrospective. His views were strangely prophetic.

He reluctantly began to take notice of a nagging back pain when his doctor advised hospital tests. The consultant returned with the results a few days later, and spoke quietly to Reg in the large, rarely used lounge. Reg listened intently, before interrupting him, and turned to face me in the adjoining chair. *"I'm fucked,"* he said, loudly.

That was the only reference he made to dying. He never mentioned it again, and nor did anyone else. He fuelled his fear and anger into the cartoon, keeping even longer hours in the den, and drawing with a vigour and single-mindedness, which was hard for us to understand. When he spoke, it was terse, with none of the humour or little observations he liked to share; he even stopped watching films. Reg continued to sketch outlines, his drawing board on knee, even while he was clearly in great discomfort. Such absolute absorption meant he could avoid everything; Canute-like, he and Andy pushed the ugly, frightening reality away.

He finally married Jean in a simple ceremony at home a few weeks before he died. As ever he took a dim view of himself, 'I will never be her knight in shining armour.' I had heard him say that before when talking about the women in his life; but perhaps there was one who thought differently — Florrie.

The media coverage following his death was extensive, and Reg would have been delighted at the praise. He would have been particularly pleased with the acknowledgements from the 'heavyweight' newspapers. A long time ago he had had ambitions to get a cartoon published in Punch magazine, after 900 attempts he made it, then he said it didn't matter anymore. I think he would have felt the same about the obituaries.

The Times called him 'One of the most syndicated cartoonists of all time'; The Independent hailed the strip as 'a comedy of recognition' and praised its fine texture of truth and lies; The Guardian commented upon how many academics tried to draw parallels between Andy and post-war life in Britain ... academics like historian E. Gombrich, who described a daily dose of Andy Capp as the X-ray of the nation's collective unconscious ... The Telegraph acknowledged the international appeal of the cartoon, despite its peculiarly regional and British origins, and wondered at the character's incorrigible idleness and brutishly funny attitudes which made him as much loved in Istanbul and Moscow as he was on Wearside, and finally, The Guardian, simply remembered Andy and Flo together against the world, in the pub or on the football pitch — a formidable duo.

Reg was given a posthumous Lifetime Achievement Award from the Cartoonists Trust, and in 2012, 14 years after his death, a bronze statue of Andy was unveiled by Jean outside The Harbour of Refuge pub on Hartlepool's headland.

... A statue, eh pet? It's nice to think the lad still goes down well, although he may be a little lonely on his own ... it's a pity Florrie can't join him. I'd miss her.

Postscript

ANDY HAS HAD a rough ride since Reg's death; Piers Morgan, the then editor of the Mirror, made no secret of detesting the cartoon, and initially it was a battle to get the statue erected with local official mutterings about "not sure if it is the image we want." But thanks to the huge stockpile of cartoons Reg left, and loyal cartoon editor Ken Layson's early efforts to mix and match them with new ones, meant that the cartoon is now back to number one position in the newspaper, and continues to generate a huge fan base.

The current popularity and spate of merchandising owes much to the team now of Lawrence Goldsmith, Roger Mahoney and Sean Garnett's dedication to recreating the characters and location, as well as interpreting Reg's unique style of humour. They freely acknowledge, however, they can never totally replicate what Reg Smythe did. "It was his creation, he was a genius and nobody can fill those shoes." Recent forays include Olympic games T-shirts, home-brew kits, an iPhone app and even, it is suggested, the possibility of animated shorts on television.

All of which would have pleased Reg enormously, but he would have struggled to let go of Andy and Florrie to anyone else; they really were his world, and increasingly it was just about them, minimal background and hardly any other characters.

I have my own favourite cartoons, of course, from the hectic, gag-driven ones of the early days to the two-hander ones of much later, just Andy and Florrie, sparring with each other, and sharing that intimate relationship with the rest of us. And I detect traces of Florrie in Andy's character; he has much of her feisty, self-willed, sod 'em approach to life. My grandmother, Florrie, was a powerful figure in Reg's life and certainly motivated his ambition, as well as influencing all his relationships with women. In this, he always seemed to be seeking a mother figure, no matter how passionate the beginning, he ultimately turned them into the mother he had always wanted, just like Andy.

I still miss visiting Reg in his den, board on knee, sketching and inking-in the outlines of Andy and Florrie, sipping tea and watching the pile of cartoons grow on the sofa, ready to be sent down to London. He was totally immersed in their world, knowing instinctively what was right for them and how they would interact, anything else was just distraction.

Although he would readily describe Andy as his dancing bear, in the end it was Reg who was lauded for dedication to his art, and presenting the world with what one obituary writer called the very first British working class anti-hero.

~ ~ ~

Reg Smythe: Creator of Andy Capp
is also available as an e-book
for Kindle, iBook, Amazon Fire, Nook and
Android e-readers. Visit
creatorspublishing.com to learn more.

∘ ∘ ∘

CREATORS PUBLISHING

We publish books.
We find compelling storytellers and
help them craft their narrative,
distributing their novels and collections
worldwide.

∘ ∘ ∘

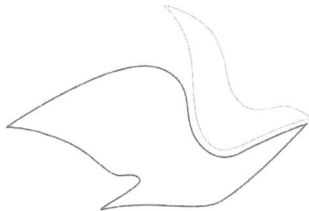

www.ingramcontent.com/pod-product-compliance
Lightning Source LLC
Chambersburg PA
CBHW031628040426
42452CB00007B/725